"An empathetic and forensic analysis that confronts the most important but hardest and most neglected question about prisons: what are they for?"
**Nick Hardwick, Royal Holloway,
University of London**

"With an ever-rising prison population, there has never been a better time to ask what prisons are for. This wide-ranging and thoughtful book, drawing on inspection experience and comparative research, points out that, despite the stated aim of rehabilitation, '[t]he vast majority of prisons are good at keeping people in and mediocre or poor at everything else'. So, prisons can and must be improved – but if we think that a massive investment in prisons is the answer to complex social problems, we are not asking the right question."
Anne Owers, previously Chief Inspector of Prisons and Chair of prison Independent Monitoring Boards

"An exceptional overview of the history and nature of imprisonment, managing to be highly comprehensive, analytically sophisticated and crystal clear."
**Ben Crewe, Prisons Research Centre,
University of Cambridge**

"Its key strength and unique contribution is an unusual fusion of experience, research and theory. Profoundly scholarly and evidence-based, it is also deeply rooted in Bhui's experience, and in his encounters with prisoners and staff inside prisons. His remarkable gift for asking normative questions (about what prisons should be) and critical and empirical questions (about what prison is and what it does) marks this book out as a compelling and important intervention. Anyone with an interest in prisons and, more generally, in punishment, should read this book, and reflect upon it deeply."

Fergus McNeill, University of Glasgow

"Bhui expertly weaves together his observations from a diversity of prisons, rich historical and social context and often overlooked perspectives to highlight the challenges facing modern carceral systems and – perhaps most uniquely – provide a compelling foundation for meaningful change."

Jordan M. Hyatt, Drexel University

"To change it, we have to understand it. Bhui's engaging, informed and critical analysis of the purpose of prisons and the impact of those who spend large parts of their lives inside them, is a significant contribution towards this aim. Students, scholars, correctional professionals, abolitionists, penal enthusiasts and liberal reformers – this book is for all of them."

Anna Eriksson, Monash University

The status quo is broken. Humanity today faces multiple interconnected challenges, some of which could prove existential. If we believe the world could be different, if we want it to be *better*, examining the purpose of what we do – and what is done in our name – is more pressing than ever.

The What Is It For? series examines the purpose of the most important aspects of our contemporary world, from religion and free speech to animal rights and the Olympics. It illuminates what these things are by looking closely at what they do.

The series offers fresh thinking on current debates that gets beyond the overheated polemics and easy polarizations. Across the series, leading experts explore new ways forward, enabling readers to engage with the possibility of real change.

Series editor: George Miller

Visit **bristoluniversitypress.co.uk/what-is-it-for** to find out more about the series.

HINDPAL SINGH BHUI OBE is Visiting Law Professor at the Centre for Criminology, University of Oxford and an Inspection Team Leader at HM Inspectorate of Prisons (HMIP). He has led various international projects to support prison and immigration detention reform and human rights-based oversight. He has trained prison staff and prison monitors in Europe, the Middle East, the Far East and Africa. He is an expert inspector for the European Committee for the Prevention of Torture and Inhuman or Degrading Treatment or Punishment (CPT), part of the Council of Europe. He has led and authored various thematic reviews on custody in England and Wales, most recently on the Experiences of Adult Black Male Prisoners and Black Prison Staff (HMIP, 2022).

WHAT ARE PRISONS FOR?

HINDPAL SINGH BHUI

Ⓑ

First published in Great Britain in 2024 by

Bristol University Press
University of Bristol
1–9 Old Park Hill
Bristol
BS2 8BB
UK
t: +44 (0)117 374 6645
e: bup-info@bristol.ac.uk

Details of international sales and distribution partners are available at
bristoluniversitypress.co.uk

British Library Cataloguing in Publication Data
A catalogue record for this book is available from the British Library

ISBN 978-1-5292-2689-8 paperback
ISBN 978-1-5292-2690-4 ePub
ISBN 978-1-5292-2691-1 ePdf

Cover design: Tom Appshaw
Bristol University Press uses environmentally
responsible print partners.
Printed and bound in Great Britain by CPI Group (UK) Ltd,
Croydon, CR0 4YY

This book contains descriptions of violence, abuse and racism that readers may find distressing.

For Liz

CONTENTS

LIST OF FIGURES

ACKNOWLEDGEMENTS

I would like to thank Keith Davies, Mary Bosworth, Joe Levenson, George Miller and Liz Dixon for their extremely helpful comments on earlier drafts. I had many thought-provoking conversations while I was writing the book, and am especially grateful to Eleanor Fellowes, Andrea Coomber, Peter Dawson, Anne Owers, Natasha Porter, Leila Ulrich, Larissa Rundle, Pia Sinha, Charlie Taylor and Jean-Sébastien Blanc. Most of all, my deepest thanks to all the people who live and work in prison, whose stories I have been so privileged to hear.

1

A JOURNEY INTO PRISONS

Prison works. It ensures that we are protected from murderers, muggers and rapists – and it makes many who are tempted to commit crime think twice ... This may mean that more people will go to prison. I do not flinch from that. We shall no longer judge the success of our system of justice by a fall in our prison population. (Michael Howard)[1]

The prison ... functions ideologically as an abstract site into which undesirables are deposited, relieving us of the responsibility of thinking about the real issues afflicting those communities from which prisoners are drawn in such disproportionate numbers. (Angela Y. Davis)[2]

First night centre was scary as I was sharing with four other prisoners and could not sleep all night, one person was suicidal and had withdrawal symptoms from ... another person was suicidal and was screaming all night ... (Anonymous prisoner)[3]

Most of us have some idea of what prisons do and how they do it, often informed by dramatic representations of them in books, films or documentaries. We carry around with us an unconscious blueprint of what prisons are, which may find resonance in one or more of the quotations that open this chapter. But, for most of us, our images of prison probably do not come from personal experience or from the evidence gathered by researchers.

My own relationship with the prison evolved from fantasy into reality over many years. As a child I lived close to a prison and found it a ready source of stories, which I thought would impress other children. One story, which may or may not have been true (I honestly can't remember), was about me spotting someone behaving strangely, seeing the police arrive and later finding out that the person was an escaped prisoner. As a child, I saw this dull story as an extraordinary personal brush with criminality, which would thrill and impress my friends. The prison of my imagination was separate and sealed off, a source of fear, strangeness and excitement, while the prisoner was a faceless threat, lacking in personality and humanity.

Oddly, it was not until I was an adult that I told anyone about something that pre-dated this story and was unambiguously true. I told it in a less sensationalized way. It was the story of a neighbour whose family I knew quite well as I went to school with his siblings. He was convicted and imprisoned for a very serious offence. I had no idea what became of him and I didn't particularly care. This story did not feel in the least bit thrilling to me as it was likely to frighten or appal rather than impress my friends. His exclusion from society led to him being excluded from my mind. This was not a story I wanted to tell because the only criminals and prisons with which I was prepared to engage were those of imagination.

Some years later, after toying with the idea of becoming a journalist, then a lawyer and then a mental health social worker, I decided to join the probation service. After two years of training, I started working as a community probation officer, and I saw my primary role as helping people to keep away from crime and move forward with their lives. I did not believe that prison was likely to help people achieve these goals and had absolutely no intention of ever working in one. Like many of my colleagues at the time, I thought of prison as representing multiple failures – by the criminal justice system, by society and by the people who had offended. At times, somewhat arrogantly, I felt I had personally failed because I had not been able to exert enough influence to keep a person out of prison. This may have been because of a badly argued court report, or my inability to find them accommodation or a drug rehabilitation placement, or just a failure to build positive professional relationships that could help me to get alongside them and encourage them.

Then, more by chance than design, I ended up working in a prison. During five years as a community probation officer, I had developed a semi-specialism in work with people with mental health problems, and HMP Wandsworth – a large local prison in south London, which was close to my home – needed someone with my background at a moment when I was looking for a change. Prison managers also wanted someone to work with the five hundred or so foreign nationals held at that time and, coincidentally, I had done some research in this area. I was excited by the challenge but surprised at the run-down, dirty and austere environment I found on starting work in this ageing Victorian prison. It was the late 1990s, and a new British government had just come to power on a wave of optimism, promising not only to be 'tough on crime', but also 'tough on the causes of crime' by supporting and strengthening communities and focusing on crime prevention.[4] But there was nothing in this vision about the role of the prison, and the optimism of the times seemed to be at odds with what I saw every day at work.

Most people came out of their cramped shared cells for no more than a few hours a day, there was very little work, education or rehabilitation, and treatment by far too many of the staff was dismissive and often verbally aggressive. This sub-group of staff, rather than the many decent ones, dominated the prison's culture. It seemed to take little effort to improve things in this context, and most prisoners were grateful for the chance to come out of their cells and have normal, respectful human interactions. I formed a small team of prisoners, prison officers and a community sector legal advisor, which provided information and support to foreign nationals. These prisoners frequently had little idea of what was going to happen to them next because of language barriers, limited legal advice, or a lack of information and competent case management from the Home Office's immigration teams.[5]

While I expected to meet many people with varying degrees of mental ill health, the lack of care and compassion for them surprised me. One of my jobs was to assess the risk of people self-harming and, along with a multi-disciplinary team, to support people in crisis over the worst points of their lives. The first few times I went to these meetings, they were held in a dirty, depressingly run-down healthcare office strewn with broken furniture – if there were too few places to sit, the doctor who chaired the meeting would usually tell the prisoner to remain standing. The prisoner would then shuffle about while describing the state of his mental health and whether he intended to kill himself. If he said he did not, he was generally ushered out of the room before, it seemed to me, he had a chance to change his mind and potentially complicate everyone's diaries. The whole process was shameful – at the time I thought it was just how all prisons were, and it was a relief when I realized that better care was delivered in many prisons by staff who fight every day to find space for compassionate professionalism.[6]

The role of race and racism in prison life was another early lesson. Like many people who grew up in 1970s and 1980s England, racism had left its mark on me, and I was attracted to the probation service partly because it felt like a safe and self-aware organization. People talked openly, if not always productively, about the impact of systemic racism in criminal justice and there was an optimism about the human capacity for change that I found exciting. Despite the efforts of many people in prisons, the prison service seemed a long way behind, both institutionally and individually.[7] I remember one prison officer who regularly tried to engage me in conversation about his favourite topic, a liberal society that he believed made endless excuses for the criminal behaviour of Black people. It was a few years after the brutal murder of Stephen Lawrence, a young Black student whose case had been mishandled by an institutionally racist police force.[8] This officer was especially irritated by what he saw as the political and institutional overreaction to the murder, and I suspect he made a beeline for me because he enjoyed the challenge of convincing or provoking someone from a minority group who was willing, perhaps too willing, to listen and debate with him. This officer was a racist – prisoners of all ethnicities worked this out very quickly and most did their best to avoid him, as did many staff. He would not, I hope, survive long in today's prison service, but in the late 1990s and early 2000s he was not much of an outlier and the burden of managing him and people like him fell mainly on prisoners.[9]

Despite such experiences I very much enjoyed my work, but after five years I was starting to feel worn out and was ready to leave. I had just been offered a job in the community when I found out that the prison inspectorate needed people with my experience. I thought it would be a good opportunity to learn more about prisons, this time across the country, and perhaps even help to change things for the better. So I eventually became an inspector with the job of understanding how prisons and immigration detention worked, to what extent they were achieving their purposes, and whether they were delivering decent treatment of and conditions for prisoners. The work is privileged, humbling and fascinating, and has had me in its grips for far longer than I planned.

I have now visited over 200 prisons and other places of detention around the world for the purposes of inspection, research or consultancy. I have spoken to thousands of prisoners and staff, and spent countless hours thinking about how prisons are run, how they affect those living within them and what that means for victims and communities. While I feel comfortable walking around prisons and enjoy talking to the people who live and work in them, I have never lost the feeling of unease and even confusion that I have about what they do and why. This book has been an opportunity to explore the roots of that discomfort and further my own education, using a mixture of personal observation, prisoners' own accounts, statistics and academic research. As we shall see, it has helped me to clarify the questions that we need to be asking, even if the answers are more elusive.

Looking inside the prison to understand its purpose

The purposes of prison are usually described as punishment, deterrence, incapacitation and rehabilitation, and all are intended to help create a safer society by reducing crime. Although the emphasis that governments around the world place on each of these goals differs, they are remarkably ubiquitous. Incarceration is a major plank of criminal justice policy for most countries. Prison populations have increased hugely since the 1970s[10] and extraordinary sums of money are spent to keep over 11.5 million people locked up.[11] You could therefore be forgiven for assuming there is overwhelming evidence that prison 'works'.

However, and at risk of jumping to the end of the story too quickly, hard evidence for this claim is lacking. If we are to understand more about the purpose of prisons, we need to look much further and deeper than official statements and dominant narratives. We must disregard simple answers and simplistic explanations which state, for example, that prisons exist to keep us safe and to reform criminals. This assertion underplays, to a staggering degree, some of the most critical questions about what prisons are for: *who* is sent to prison and *why* them?

The first of these questions is much easier to answer than the second, but both are laden with political and historical complexity. For now, suffice to say that we can start to determine a great deal about purpose from an analysis of the patterns of imprisonment around the world. In some countries, prisons are often used to hold and deny power to those who oppose dominant political groups. In the wealthier societies of what is often called the 'Global North' or, more narrowly, 'the West', prisons are disproportionately filled with minority ethnic groups and foreign nationals, while prisons everywhere hold large numbers of poor, socially disadvantaged, and mentally and physically unwell people.

Noting these patterns is not to deny the importance of individual agency and the power that people have to make choices, nor does it necessarily mean that prisons perform no useful function. But I believe that a deeper analysis will help us to understand why certain groups of people are more often in situations where they make choices that lead to prison, and it also helps to make sense of the many and vociferous theoretical critiques of prison.

Another dimension too often lacking from debates about prisons is an understanding of the inner life of the prison community, where the apparently little things are as important as the big picture. Prisons are places where big projects like rebuilding relationships and changing lives are talked about endlessly and daily challenges, like healthy sexual expression and the shame of going to the toilet in front of strangers, are usually unspoken. Prisons are places of extremes: tremendous sadness and the pain of isolation exist alongside the joy of having a family visit, achieving early release or experiencing the comfort and support of fellow prisoners or staff. They represent seemingly perpetual failures and the constant promise of redemption. We must listen to prisoners and analyse these dimensions of experience to understand what they can tell us about the purpose of prisons.

The power of prison as an idea means that other forms of involuntary detention are moulded around the prison paradigm, but are more insidious because they are less regulated and less visible; for example, detention of people assessed as dangerous but who have committed no crime, or immigration detention. I will not address other forms of detention in detail here but they provide some insight into the long reach of carceral ideology. Disciplinary power also extends beyond closed institutions, and we will consider the thinking of Michel Foucault, the French philosopher who famously analysed the dispersed nature of social control and suggested that prison was merely the most prominent among many forms of discipline.

What *should* prisons be for?

Nearly everyone thinks that change is needed in relation to prisons, whether they are abolitionists who want to be rid of them, penal enthusiasts who want more, or liberal reformers who want fewer. Enthusiasts may want harsher conditions or join liberal reformers in advocating for better conditions. In broad terms, both abolitionists and liberal reformers tend to be adherents of academic research and may lay claim to a degree of 'expertise', which drives their vision of the future. Penal enthusiasts are more likely to advocate a 'common sense' perspective, which is generally out of step with the weight of academic research but far more closely aligned to government policy in most countries. They may accept that the prison and the systems of punishment in which it sits have shortcomings, but are more interested in the delivery of punishment, retribution and short-term incapacitation, often stressing the importance of focusing on victims' needs. These are obviously very crude categorizations, but they can provide a helpful route into the complex debate about penal reform.

Supporters of liberal reform may point to the Nordic countries, which imprison fewer people than most of the rest of Europe, hold them in better conditions, and are more successful in helping prisoners to maintain links to their communities, while achieving consistently lower rates of recidivism (repeat offending).[12] So-called 'Nordic exceptionalism' suggests that more equal societies with strong welfare states and more cultural homogeneity are likely to be most successful in reducing recidivism. Prisons cannot, in this view, be considered in isolation from the rest of society any more than individuals can be seen as untethered rational actors uninfluenced by their environment. We are also forced to consider whether prisons are *intrinsically* problematic institutions given, for example, the degree to which they reflect social inequality and disadvantage, and their explicit use to control political opponents in some parts of the world.

Liberal reformers and, to an extent, abolitionists tend to have a more positive view of people – they are more likely to trust the ability of individuals to change and of society to manage and control poor behaviours without the use of confinement. Instead, they see reduction of disadvantage and promotion of equality as more important keys to crime reduction. The arguably more dominant perspective is based on a less positive view of humanity – that is, that without the control and deterrence imposed by the punitive state, and its expression through the banishment represented by the prison, people's worst behaviours cannot be deterred or controlled. People are responsible for their actions, and the known predisposing factors to imprisonment, such as poverty and other forms of social disadvantage, are likely to be seen as individual failings. Even if there is an acceptance of societal responsibility for crime, this is likely to be considered irrelevant to decisions about whether to imprison or not. The problem exists and needs a response, and the common abolitionist argument that prisons are a means of managing disadvantaged people has little traction.[13]

Prison enthusiasts may be more concerned with the symbolic power of the prison and how it makes them *feel* than they are with the evidence of effectiveness in reducing crime. By extension, they may give more credence to the feelings of dread that the idea of prison is assumed to induce in potential offenders. In a withering attack on arguments for the existence of prisons, the Norwegian sociologist Thomas Mathiesen argues that 'we have prisons ... because there exists a pervasive and persistent ideology of prison in our society'.[14] In other words, prisons are a powerful *idea*. As we sketch the rise of this institution, we will start to uncover why and how the idea of prison has gained such a grip on the imagination.

As we critically examine the prison futures that these protagonists may have in mind, we will ask some big questions, including, 'To what extent is the story of imprisonment the story of racialized control?' Race is so central to the use of imprisonment that it cannot be decoupled from the prison debate in the Global North. As the world's most enthusiastic incarcerator, the US provides a particularly valuable case study of the drivers and effects of advanced carceral policies. In her influential work on imprisonment in the US, the activist and academic Michelle Alexander argues that the penal system is indeed a sophisticated form of racialized control, which functions in a way that is similar to the 'Jim Crow' segregation laws and, in effect, perpetuates the legacy of slavery.[15]

A more generalized view of this argument is prominent in abolitionist accounts, which stress the prison's alleged role in exercising control over marginalized people. Abolitionists generally advocate for fundamental social change which will eventually render prisons unnecessary as problems such as inequality, racial and gender-based discrimination and violence are addressed. Individuals and their culpability for crime are less visible to abolitionists than iniquitous systems. They have mounted fierce defences against the accusation that theirs is a utopian dream. For example, British academic Joe Sim argues that the seekers of the ideally reformed prison, which is decent, humane and effective, are the real utopian dreamers.[16] Abolitionists believe that we need a more ambitious vision than that offered by liberal reformers to see meaningful positive change. We will therefore explore the extent to which the prison is about managing marginalized and unwanted people, and whether this should matter to us.

Another key question is, 'Why are prisons full of men?' Only 7 per cent of the world's prison population is female.[17] While the number of women prisoners has been increasing, the lower rate at which they are incarcerated is nevertheless startling. We will consider the history of women's imprisonment and the ways that states everywhere seem to find alternative ways of ensuring conformity and controlling women's behaviour.

About this book

We will start this exploration by looking in the next two chapters at the development of the modern prison in different parts of the world, before considering, in Chapter 4, the phenomenon of mass imprisonment, and the US experience in particular. As I searched for ways into the question of purpose I found myself delving further into prison histories than I first intended, and I hope readers will see why these are so important. As the prison's purpose also reveals itself through the backgrounds and experiences of prisoners, in Chapters 5 and 6 we will discuss the details of prison life through a combination of research and case studies. The book concludes with a discussion of possible futures, including different approaches to reform and alternative models of punishment.

I have not written this book as a memoir, but I have included personal observations throughout, and hope the fusion of experience, research and theory will be a new and unusual way for readers to enter the world of prisons. There is no need to start at the beginning – each chapter is reasonably self-contained and readers should feel free to start anywhere they wish.

A final point: opinions about criminal justice and prisons tend to flow freely and strongly, often driven by powerful feelings, ranging from outrage, fear and confusion, to compassion and concern. Bias confirmation is simple to find, and facts, or lack of them, are easily obscured. I will do my best to avoid lecturing readers. My intention is to provide information and to guide, and I will not set out to argue in favour of established positions and marshal facts in support of them. Inevitably I will not always succeed, but I hope that effort will keep engaged readers from all persuasions, and promote informed and critical thought about the way that prisons are used and experienced.

2

A BRIEF HISTORY OF IMPRISONMENT IN THE WEST

All of the dominant ideological reconfigurations of official penal discourse over the last 400 years, have, in different ways, managed to avoid the question 'What are prisons for?' (Pat Carlen and Anne Worrall)[1]

Imagine you were living somewhere in the Roman Empire in the early first millennium, and you punched a Roman official. If you lacked wealth or influence, the chances are that you would be thrown into a filthy communal underground dungeon to await trial and/or execution. Your friends and family would bring you food and you might be chained and tortured. If you were continually reincarnated during the following two thousand years and retained the urge to assault state officials, your experience of prison would change relatively little until the eighteenth century, at which point something odd would happen. Instead of going to prison to wait for punishment, prison would *become* your punishment. And rather than merely punishing your body, jailers would take an interest in influencing your mind. The conditions of your confinement would change in line with these new purposes of imprisonment: for example, you would have a single cell at last to encourage silent contemplation and religious awakening, and you would be expected to work to develop self-discipline and maybe generate income for the state.

Fast forward to the twenty-first century and, sitting in your prison cell, you might reflect on what had so far been a 300-hundred-year struggle not only to punish but also to incapacitate and reform you through imprisonment. You would have lost your single cell long ago with the onset of mass imprisonment and overcrowding, and you might wonder at the obsession with prison in popular culture. In the wake of colonialism and post-colonial migration, you may have noticed that many of your fellow inmates were now black or brown, and some would be foreign. You might also wonder why the prison is holding so many people who are mentally and physically ill, dependent on drugs and alcohol, or neurodiverse. The promise of 'rehabilitation' would be repeated at every turn, but you probably wouldn't feel that society wants to welcome you back. You may well be in a state of deep confusion as to what your jailers are trying to achieve and why.

What follows will, I hope, help to make sense of these changes, with the caveat that this is a selective and non-linear history beset by the common problems of all historical inquiry.[2] There was very little empirical research during key periods in the development of the modern prison, and first-hand prisoner accounts before the mid-twentieth century were scarce, albeit in some cases profoundly insightful.[3] We are largely unable to hear the voices of the people who lived and worked in these institutions, and the experiences of women and minority ethnic groups are even more obscured. Diverse prison voices are largely absent from the commentaries of the eighteenth and nineteenth centuries produced by prominent figures like John Howard, Alexis de Tocqueville and Charles Dickens, and in the work of highly regarded recent commentators such as Michel Foucault and Michael Ignatieff. Nevertheless, if we are to understand the present and assess possible futures for the prison, it is important to critically explore existing histories, while acknowledging that some areas are, and are likely to remain, hidden from view.

The rise of the modern prison

People have been subject to the public imposition of involuntary confinement for many thousands of years.[4] We know prisons existed in the ancient empires of Egypt, Rome, Persia and Mesopotamia, where their purpose was usually to hold people until an often brutal sentence could be carried out[5] – and so it remained for centuries. Although prisons were sometimes used to punish, until the late eighteenth century they were overwhelmingly a short-term measure for those awaiting trial or a sentence of death or slavery, or to hold enemies of the state, prisoners of war and those awaiting transportation to the colonies. Another prominent category of prisoner was the debtor: in eighteenth-century Britain, debtors comprised 60 per cent of prisoners recorded in prison reformer John Howard's survey of English prisons in the 1770s,[6] and 69 per cent of those in Scotland's largest prison between 1720 and 1770.[7] They were usually held for far longer than those accused of crimes, and were the only people for whom the prison was clearly a punishment.[8] As one historian has put it, these prisons could be seen 'less as tools to attack criminality, and more as forms of economic sanction'.[9] It was not until the eighteenth and, especially, the nineteenth centuries that imprisonment began the journey to its current boom status, gathering the social and political meaning that it now embodies. It is debatable if we should even use the term 'prison' for the collection of dungeons, lock-ups and prison ships (known as 'prison hulks') that existed until that time essentially as holding pens devoid of any greater purpose.

The prison in its modern sense as an institution intended to 'correct' behaviours (thus 'correctional facility') first emerged in North America and Western Europe. The early history of incarceration in the US is dominated by two famous approaches to imprisonment, the so-called Pennsylvania and Auburn models, which differed mainly in that the former imposed strict solitary confinement. The word 'penitentiary' derives

Figure 2.1: Mamertine Prison, Rome, constructed c. 700 BCE

from the Latin term for 'a place of penitence', which is what the American Quakers in Pennsylvania, who coined this term, wanted these new prisons to be. The imposition of total isolation and silence would, it was assumed, force prisoners into self-reflection and repentance of sin and encourage social conformity. There was, however, a major problem: this solitary regime commonly resulted in mental, physical and emotional breakdown and self-harm. Charles Dickens was a shocked witness to this model of punishment during his 1842 visit to the Eastern State Penitentiary in Pennsylvania. He spoke to many of the prisoners held there and gives an early indication of the confusion of purpose that has surrounded the prison ever since:

> In its intention, I am well convinced that it is kind, humane, and meant for reformation; but I am persuaded that those

who devised this system of Prison Discipline, and those
benevolent gentlemen who carry it into execution, do not
know what it is that they are doing. I believe that very
few men are capable of estimating the immense amount
of torture and agony which this dreadful punishment,
prolonged for years, inflicts upon the sufferers ...[10]

While the Auburn approach did not abandon the belief in silent reflection, it modified the Pennsylvania model by providing much more activity, and opportunities to eat and work in groups. It quickly became the more popular approach, perhaps because it was also cheaper – ensuring total isolation had proven difficult and costly, as well as torturous for those subjected to it.

Meanwhile, in England, the first national penitentiary, Millbank, was opened in 1816 and was almost immediately beset by problems despite the huge sums of money spent on it. These included rampant disease, frequent prisoner riots, shaky physical foundations (the whole prison was literally sinking) and a poor design, which meant that prisoners who were meant to engage in silent contemplation could communicate easily with each other through the ventilation system.[11] Millbank was condemned as a costly failure and returned to one of the older purposes of prison when it became a holding pen for those awaiting transportation. It exemplifies well the persistent theme in prison history of huge investment for unclear rewards.

A new prison, Pentonville, opened in north London in 1842 with a radial design that made it easier to

Figure 2.2: Millbank Prison, c. 1820

observe each wing from the centre. It quickly became the model for other prisons in the UK and throughout the British empire. It was rather more effective than Millbank at imposing solitude, hard labour and religious indoctrination, and its sturdiness is evidenced by the fact that it is still standing today, holding over 1,000 people. Little else can be said about its effectiveness given that it has long been regarded as one of the worst prisons in England and Wales, despite the considerable efforts of its leaders and staff.[12] I was last there in 2022, when it seemed to me a cramped and crumbling relic. Many of the cells have changed little since the 1800s, apart from the installation of a toilet next to prisoners' beds, and the radical loss of privacy and dignity as prisoners now share cells originally designed for one person.

Figure 2.3: HMP Pentonville cell with improvised toilet screening, 2022

Figure 2.4: HMP Pentonville cell for people spending their first night in custody, 2022

A triumph of humanitarianism?

The increased use of prisons from the 1800s came about because influential people started believing that confinement could be both a punishment *and* a means of moral rehabilitation. What happened to bring about this fundamental shift? The more orthodox explanation – and the most clearly evidenced – is that the European Enlightenment inspired a strain of humanitarianism that challenged the legitimacy of torture and execution for more serious crimes and sought more effective ways of combatting less serious ones. People began to place a greater value on moral correction rather than on either brutal punishment or light-touch reparative approaches to wrongdoing. Many reformers were also inspired by religious conviction to offer criminals – or force them to accept – the chance of redemption. Meanwhile, utilitarian thinkers[13] saw an opportunity to make better use of the labour and energy of criminals by requiring them to work.

Torture, execution, humiliation, the infliction of terrible conditions and transportation were all incompatible with both utilitarian objectives and the liberal sensibilities of Europe's growing middle classes. Hence there was a move away from capital and corporal punishment, and towards efforts to improve conditions in prisons. It was hoped that they might as a consequence become suitable places for reforming people who were now held long enough for attempts at rehabilitation to take place.

The emerging contradictions in the purposes of imprisonment come increasingly into focus when you consider that at the same time prisons were supposed to remain grim, scary and austere enough to make them a feared punishment which was 'capable of reconciling deterrence and reform, terror and humanity'.[14]

The second main explanation sees a more sinister purpose to this apparent humanitarianism. 'Revisionist' thinkers believe, in essence, that the changing approach to imprisonment was the result of the powerful and privileged discovering more sophisticated forms of social control. They place more emphasis on the fact that in the eighteenth century, 'the spectacular punishments originally intended as deterrent warnings to potential lawbreakers were increasingly being seen by the hungry masses as illegitimate weapons of repression'.[15]

Concerned by the threat of rebellion against state authority, governments looked for more subtle ways of controlling and keeping order in society and, also spurred on by the need for a more self-disciplined and reliable workforce during a period of rapid industrialization,[16] prison seemed a good all-round solution. The value of prison labour became even more apparent because of a widespread shortage of workers, which led to prisoners being forced to work both inside the prison and, eventually, outside it. A particularly infamous work scheme is the convict lease system in the southern United States after the American Civil War, whereby, in an unsubtle echo of slavery, the forced labour of usually Black imprisoned men was sold to private contractors. The convict lease system provided much-needed income to Southern states and was a 'political tool that enabled wealthy and elite white Southerners to maintain the racial and economic systems Emancipation was intended to dismantle'.[17] This special form of slavery continued until well into the twentieth century.

The reforms did mean that prisoners were now unlikely to be mutilated or killed and less likely to be forced to live in filthy and degrading conditions. But many more people were now experiencing prison than had previously been subject to violent but swift state-sanctioned punishment, and they were held for longer. Imprisonment continued to increase despite a widespread belief by the mid-nineteenth century, in both Europe and the US, that it was neither particularly humane nor effective at preventing reoffending. This adds weight, as one historian has argued, to 'the revisionist argument that the main purpose of prison is the exercise of power'.[18] But what does it mean to 'exercise power' through the prison?

Foucault and the development of social control theories

The French philosopher Michel Foucault has attained something approaching criminological rockstar status. His writings include perhaps the most famous revisionist history, *Discipline and Punish*,[19] which was first published in French in 1975 and has become a much praised (and occasionally derided) touchstone for subsequent analyses. In the famously visceral opening to his book, Foucault describes contemporary reports of the particularly gruesome public execution of the would-be assassin of Louis XV, Robert-François Damiens:

> the flesh will be torn from his breasts, arms, thighs and calves with red-hot pincers, his right hand, holding the knife with which he committed the said parricide, burnt with sulphur, and, on those places where the flesh will be torn away, poured molten lead, boiling oil, burning resin, wax and sulphur melted together and then his body drawn and quartered by four horses and his limbs and body consumed by fire, reduced to ashes and his ashes thrown to the winds.[20]

Foucault had a more subtle objective than shocking his readers with the horrors of punishment in mid-eighteenth-century France: he wanted to question the orthodox view that these extreme horrors were replaced by something that was unquestionably good. Descriptions of the torture that had apparently been consigned to history might distract people from the fact that different ways to inflict pain were being developed, despite and because of the rise of the prison:

> imprisonment – mere loss of liberty – has never functioned without a certain additional element of punishment that certainly concerns the body itself: rationing of food, sexual deprivation, corporal punishment, solitary confinement ... There remains, therefore, a trace of 'torture' in the modern mechanisms of criminal justice – a trace that has not been entirely overcome, but which is enveloped, increasingly, by the non-corporal nature of the penal system.[21]

Foucault makes a link here to the work on the 'pains of imprisonment' pioneered by Gresham Sykes in the 1950s (see Chapter 6), and he had little time for those who argued that humanitarian impulses lay behind the growth of imprisonment; he instead asserts that prison emerged as merely the most prominent of many new techniques of social control.

Central to Foucault's thinking is the idea of 'capillary power': power which is now everywhere rather than wielded by a sovereign. This power defines what is normal or deviant, and what is knowledge and truth. It is present in eighteenth-century institutions such as prisons, schools and mental hospitals, which are part of what he described as a 'carceral archipelago', with prisons at the apex. These institutions now largely rejected the use of violence to control people, and instead deployed surveillance and assessment to define how people were classified and how they should behave, even encouraging them to exercise self-discipline without compulsion, because they felt they were being watched, even when they were not: 'Prison continues, on those who are entrusted to it, a work begun elsewhere, which the whole of society pursues on each individual through innumerable mechanisms of discipline.'[22]

The internalization of discipline is encouraged by forced routines such as the scheduling of when you get up and go to sleep, or when you eat and associate with others. This process is assisted by the growth of new disciplines such as criminology and psychiatry, which helped to classify populations according to risk, and shift punishment from a swift attack on the body to a slower, more deliberate entanglement of the mind. The evolution of probation and other community sentences could be seen as another illustration of this process.

An extreme example of such 'ideological containment'[23] can be seen in the nineteenth-century American South, where a physician, Dr Samuel Cartwright, discovered new diseases, including 'rascality' and one that he called 'drapetomania'. This latter affliction caused 'the negro to run away from service' and 'is as much a disease of the mind as any other species of mental alienation, and much more curable, as a general rule. With the advantages of proper medical advice, strictly followed,

Figure 2.5: 'The runaway', picture used in handbills and newspaper advertisements

this troublesome practice that many negroes have of running away, can be almost entirely prevented.'[24]

However ridiculous such pronouncements seem today, Cartwright was taken seriously by many of his contemporaries.[25] 'Scientific racism' helped to legitimate control of Black people under the cover of medicine, and imprisonment was just one manifestation of this system of control.

In its location of the prison within an oppressive socio-political order that reinforces inequality, Foucault's work is a variation on the classic Marxist explanation for the purpose of prison. This view states, in essence, that penal power is a tool of the capitalist project, helping the state to control surplus labour.[26] This analysis remains influential, and readers will see echoes of it in various parts of this book, including, for example, the discussions of Russian prisons in Chapter 3, and of mass imprisonment in Chapter 4.

While Foucault identifies different methods or 'technologies' of social control developed to contain the lower classes and protect middle-class property interests, he does not align himself with Marxist analyses that focus on class oppression any more than he accepts liberal ideas of linear progress from barbarism to enlightened humanitarianism. Instead, he invites people to use his work as a 'toolkit', drawing on analytical frameworks and ideas that are useful and disregarding ones that are not. What his work means to me is encouragement to think beyond orthodoxies and to question previous certainties. Like a good teacher,

Foucault provides a framework for independent analysis rather than neat answers.

Social control theorists continue to increase our understanding of society and the role of the penal system. For example, David Garland's work on the US and the UK includes an exploration of how the concept of rehabilitation has largely refocused on risk management and control rather than supporting individuals to change.[27] Garland laments the attempts to create social order through the penal system, rather than resolving the problems of economic marginalization and social exclusion: 'Instead of working to build the complex institutions of governance and integration needed to regulate and unify today's social and economic order, these penal policies have set up a division between those groups who can be allowed to live in deregulated freedom, and those who must be heavily controlled.'[28]

Social control is, of course, not necessarily a bad thing – ordered societies cannot function without sets of rules and practices that limit individual freedoms. Sociologist Pat Carlen has made a helpful distinction between the benign institutional practice of social control which is 'in the interests of the collectivity's proclaimed ideals of social and criminal justice' and what she terms 'antisocial control'. She summarizes this as:

> a variety of malign institutionalised practices that may either set limits to individual action by favouring one set of citizens at the expense of another so as to subvert equal

opportunities ideologies in relation to gender, race and
class (or other social groupings); or (in societies without
equal opportunities ideologies) set limits to individual
action in ways that are antisocial because they atrophy an
individual's social contribution and do so on the grounds of
either biological attributes or exploitative social relations.[29]

Unless we take a step back to look at histories and
patterns, the existence of control mechanisms can
be largely invisible; and control that evades critical
scrutiny becomes dangerous, potentially spawning
Carlen's 'malign institutionalised practices'. The big
picture insights of social control theorists help us move
towards a deeper analysis of criminal justice practices
and throw light on the reasons for the purpose of prison
remaining so contested.

Others have argued that the religious reformers
of the eighteenth and nineteenth centuries played
a central role in expanding the modern prison.[30] In
this view, Christian reformers could not save souls
in the chaotic and disordered environment presented
by the prisons of the day, and this led to safer, more
disciplined and therefore more legitimate institutions.
In short, once again we see prison reform with benign
motives harnessed to a wider purpose of sophisticated
social control.

Most commentators on prison history now have
a position somewhere between the Foucauldian and
humanitarian, and thinking continues to develop in
response to the challenges laid down by revisionist
historians. Notably the Canadian historian and

former politician Michael Ignatieff, one of the original revisionist school, quickly and thoughtfully critiqued his own position. Although he retains his central charge that traditional histories lack insight into the social control functions of prison, Ignatieff acknowledges that the revisionist position has over-schematized prison history and that the intentions behind the new institution should be seen in a more nuanced light. Thus, 'historical reality is more complex than the revisionists assumed [and] reformers were more humanitarian than revisionists have made them out to be'.[31]

As is the case with most grand theories, social control arguments can be criticized, and frequently are, for privileging sweeping socio-political analysis over individual agency. But they should encourage healthy discomfort and creative reflection among criminal justice policy makers and practitioners. Foucault's writings have come to spearhead a larger body of work that fundamentally challenges the idea that the prison and other agencies of law and order evolved primarily to reduce harm to individuals or society.

Discovering women in prison history

Prison was created by and for men, and until the protests of nineteenth-century reformers such as Elizabeth Fry and John Howard, imprisoned women were simply held alongside men, often in worse material conditions, and subject to routine abuse and exploitation: 'The governors of the London Bridewell ... ran their prison as a highly profitable brothel ... Those who would not prostitute themselves "voluntarily" were coerced by threats and beatings to join in this unorthodox form of prison employment.'[32]

The situation was very similar in the colonies of European empires, where women were also usually held with men until quite late in colonial history, experienced the worst conditions of detention and were 'forced to endure promiscuity and sexual abuses from both prisoners and guards'.[33]

The relative invisibility of women is not particularly surprising given the greater challenges to policy makers of controlling the more numerous, less well-disciplined and substantially more violent male offenders. Until the mid-nineteenth century, the predominant approach to female criminality was to see it as a deviation from the presumed feminine norm, 'a highly artificial notion of the ideal woman [as] an exemplary moral being', as Lucia Zedner puts it.[34] Prison regimes therefore focused on 'restoring' women to this idealized state of femininity, which we see in Dickens' saccharine description of women he came across in Eastern State Penitentiary:

In the silence and solitude of their lives, they had grown to be quite beautiful. Their looks were very sad, and might have moved the sternest visitor to tears ... One was a young girl ... She was very penitent and quiet; had come to be resigned, she said (and I believe her) ... raising her eyes, and meeting that glimpse of freedom over-head, she burst into tears.[35]

This romanticized view of women's innate but all too corruptible gentility and morality is connected to one of the theories that attempt to explain why women are less visible in crime statistics and the criminal justice system than men: this theory states in essence that the state has found a plethora of informal ways to influence the thoughts and regulate the behaviour of women outside the formal criminal justice system, and that ideologies of gender and family are among the most effective.[36] At the same time, women who do not live up to this image have been considered to be, writes Zedner, 'even more depraved than any criminal man', a 'dualistic view of women [that] had its roots in Christian imagery of the female as madonna and whore'.[37] The confidence of the state and society in their ability to impose control through these enforced identities may be why women have always been less visible in the criminal justice system and in criminological research compared to men, notwithstanding intense public and media interest in women who lean towards the 'whore' and/or commit the most serious crimes.[38]

The rise of the ambitious modern prison encouraged reformers to see these 'fallen' women as capable of being restored to their prescribed gender roles through rehabilitation; indeed, in US reformatories they were sent to prison for *longer* than men who had committed similar offences to allow the state to deliver time-consuming moral reformation rather than proportionate punishment.[39] Racism was as visible as ever in this endeavour: punishment for white women was, as Angela Davis puts it, 'designed ideologically to reform', while women of colour were generally segregated from white women, more likely to be sent to men's prisons, and subject to systems of punishment such as convict leasing and other 'realms of public punishment that made no pretense of offering them femininity'.[40]

With the rising popularity of the idea that innate and inheritable characteristics led to crime, women's offending became an increasing preoccupation in the nineteenth century, 'not least,' as Zedner writes, 'because, in their role as mothers, they were identified as the biological source of crime and degeneracy'.[41] The pressure for longer sentences came not only from the reformers but also, in the late nineteenth and early twentieth centuries, the increasingly influential eugenicists, who were keen to limit the ability of 'inferior' women to reproduce and supported enforced sterilization across Europe and the US.[42] A belief in the potential of medical solutions for women's criminality was layered onto ideas about their moral weaknesses, leading to a focus, through the rise of psychiatry, on their mental inadequacy – women started to be seen more as 'mad' rather than bad, which expanded the ways in which their behaviours could be controlled. As Pat Carlen and Anne Worrall put it, in addition to the normal physical security and discipline of men's prisons, women were 'psychologically interpellated [i.e. identified] (if not always constrained) by the triple disciplines of feminisation, domesticisation and medicalisation'.[43]

Patriarchal structures and misogyny are apparent in what is criminalized and how it is punished. Women

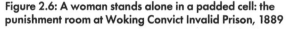

Figure 2.6: A woman stands alone in a padded cell: the punishment room at Woking Convict Invalid Prison, 1889

are imprisoned for 'crimes of immorality', such as breaches of male-imposed dress codes, extra-marital sex or adultery,[44] and most countries criminalize the distinctly female 'crime' of abortion, which in some jurisdictions might even lead to a life sentence.[45]

Today, women comprise about 7 per cent of the world's prisoners, but their number is rising at a rate that far outstrips men's imprisonment: between 2000 and 2022, the number of women in prison grew by almost 60 per cent, compared to 22 per cent for men;[46] in England and Wales the female population is predicted to increase by about 30 per cent between 2020 and 2026.[47] This acceleration may mean that women are committing more serious crime, but it also suggests loosening bonds of social control and a resort to the 'hard' form of control represented by the prison.[48]

It is clear that prison history is not a dry exercise in stacking up facts about the linear evolution of an institution – it is a history of ideas and social transformations, which have led to changes in the way that societies choose to impose social order and exercise authority and control. Like prison reform, it can only be understood by looking at the social and political context in which these institutions have existed, and working out how and why governments have used them. They represent a choice, resulting from policy decisions taken by states at different points in time and for a variety of reasons – punishing criminal behaviour was only one of those reasons and, until comparatively recently, was hardly an objective of prison at all.

The position of women and the arguments of the social control theorists may become clearer when we look at the creation of the prison in other parts of the world, especially colonized countries. It is to these distinct histories that we will now turn.

3

THE EMERGENCE OF PRISON AROUND THE WORLD

Over the years, the justifications for imprisonment have become more and more complex, contradictory and, in some cases, only eccentrically related to the punishment of crime. (Pat Carlen and Anne Worrall)[1]

The prison has evolved in such different circumstances across the world that there is an understandable tendency for scholars to focus either on North America and Europe, which invented the modern prison and has produced most thinking, research and knowledge about it; or to stick narrowly to accounts that explore the unique dynamics of imprisonment in individual countries. We clearly cannot talk about a single coherent world prison history, but it is possible to examine how the idea and ideology of the modern prison have tumbled outwards into the world. Just as importantly, we can learn a great deal about the purpose of prison in one jurisdiction by understanding how it developed in another.

I have chosen an eclectic mix of countries to discuss in this chapter: Kenya as a formerly colonized country; Japan as an independent nation; and Russia, which is something of an outlier and an intriguing case study of a powerful country with a tendency to use prison explicitly to pursue economic and political goals. Another reason for choosing these countries is because, to varying degrees, they reflect the origins of Western prisons and provide insight into aspects of them that have become obscured over time.

The colonial prison

[The African prison] is a holdover from colonial times, a European import designed to isolate and punish political opponents, exercise racial superiority, and administer capital and corporal punishment. (Jeremy Sarkin)[2]

Before the era of European colonization, prisons in much of Africa were used similarly to those in Europe and the US, that is for temporary control and incapacitation rather than punishment, and some societies found no use for the prison at all. In pre-colonial West Africa, small-scale societies without a strong central authority or government often chained criminals out in the open to await their fate.[3] Most offences were settled through mediation and reparation, and more serious crimes resulted in exile, execution or enslavement. There was no obvious clamour for new forms of punishment or new mechanisms to exercise control of populations.

If the prison had then proceeded to evolve in Africa as in Europe – that is, as a result of changing attitudes, humanitarian aspirations and/or the recognition that it was a useful tool for controlling those who posed a challenge to the predominant social order – one might assume ideologies of rehabilitation and reform to have become similarly embedded and to influence the subsequent growth of the prison. But where Foucault and other thinkers revealed the role of the European and American prison in protecting the interests of the powerful, in colonial Africa there was no need for such a sophisticated analysis.

It is not in dispute that the African prison first emerged as a stark and brutal tool of imperial control and discipline, unencumbered by humanitarian and religious ideologies of rehabilitation or redemption, or liberal sensibilities that baulked at the idea of torture. The colonial prison was created to maintain colonial rule, not to reform criminals or replace archaic punishments. It used whatever tools it could muster to reach that goal, including racist demonization of Africans considered too sub-human and savage to qualify for the humanitarian concerns that influenced changes in European penal policy. Punishments inflicted on the body continued, and while European prisons were replacing extreme bodily assault and phasing out residual practices of corporal punishment, torture was becoming increasingly entrenched in colonial prisons.[4] The prison supplemented, rather than replaced, the public violence[5] that Foucault so memorably described in France.

In common with most other regions of sub-Saharan Africa, there is no evidence of pre-colonial prisons in Kenya, but after the British took control in 1895, a rapid building programme led to 30 prisons being established by 1911 and over the following 20 years that number more than doubled to 63.[6] Many prisoners were convicted of minor offences classified as illegal activity with reference to variants of English common and criminal law that had little meaning to the Kenyan population.[7] Whereas European and US systems promoted work as self-improvement – even if the reality was often more exploitative – in Africa the explicit objective was to bolster the coffers of colonizing powers through forced prison labour: 'inmates worked at minimal expense for white colonists in both the public and private sectors. Labor circulated between "free" society, which required Africans to perform forced labor, and prisons, which sent those arrested for violating forced labor service to work for private employers.'[8]

The use of prison for political repression is also reflected in the imprisonment of many thousands of people in Kenya during the Mau Mau rebellion against colonial rule in the 1950s. At that time, over 85,000 people were incarcerated to help to keep the British in power, with numbers falling dramatically after independence in 1963 to around 13,000.

The simplicity and clarity of African incarceration policy objectives meant that there was less evidence

Figure 3.1: British colonial prisons officer outside Fort Jesus Prison, Mombasa, Kenya, 1942

of the subtleties of Foucault's capillary power. There was no need to mask the colonial's prison role in oppression, nor to shy away from the value of racism to the colonial project. The colonial prison therefore provides a clearer example than we find in the more conceptually layered prison of the West, of themes that philosophers and historians have explored at length, especially racialized control and economic gain.

The relationship between racism, imprisonment and colonialism

'Race' and 'whiteness' are biologically meaningless terms, invented only in the seventeenth century as a way for colonists and slave-owners to justify the subjugation and enslavement of 'non-white' people.[9] Classifying people according to the social construct of race was a way to help neutralize reservations about exploiting others for profit and supported the use of prison to enforce compliance with the colonial project. Africans were, as historian Florence Bernault puts it, seen as a 'delinquent race',[10] unworthy of concern or justice as it would be understood in the West.

Before the invention of race, colonists and slave-owners were more likely to think of themselves as 'Christian' than 'white'. Historian Katharine Gerbner's work on the Caribbean shows how increasing numbers of enslaved Black people were baptized, making it more likely that they could aspire to political power and freedom. Their Christian identity undermined the narrative of irredeemable inferiority and, as a result, 'slave owners gradually replaced the term "Christian" with the word "white" in their law books', an intentional and strategic step to erect further barriers to equality and freedom.[11] Racism was therefore a consequence of slavery, not the cause of it.

We see similar processes in other parts of the colonial world. For example, historian Peter Zinoman's detailed study shows how racism was an essential building block of the repressive colonial prison in Indochina, and helped to ensure that Enlightenment thinking about improving prisons' conditions and offering rehabilitation gained little traction. Encouraged by contemporary criminological theorizing about the unique nature of 'yellow criminality', French colonial bureaucrats came to see 'native' prisoners as 'intrinsically less susceptible' to reformative influences.[12] In this context, it made perfect sense that Vietnamese prisons should repress and control rather than reform. Such rationalizations led to Vietnamese prisoners being kept in overcrowded, violent and insanitary conditions while Europeans incarcerated in the same country were in individual cells and had far better treatment.[13] Racism was therefore an enabler of the worst forms of imprisonment in colonized countries. As we shall see in Chapter 4, this philosophy is arguably still visible in the West's disproportionate use of incarceration to manage perceived racialized threat.

Reforming the colonial prison

Although African states tend to imprison fewer people than in other parts of the world,[14] they have absorbed the prison into their societies and often allowed it to continue as a place of degradation today.[15] The colonial legacy has been hard to shift partly because the prison is just as valuable to leaders of independent nations to enforce social order as it was for the colonials. Good governance, political and economic stability, and strong institutions of state promote social inclusion and should reduce crime and imprisonment. But the poverty, uneven development and inequality of most post-colonial societies instead breeds a form of 'heavy control',[16] which displaces necessarily complex but far more useful institutions of governance and integration.

In the context of widespread economic and social problems, prison reform is also unlikely to be a priority. In eighteenth-century Europe, one of the challenges faced by reformers was that poverty was so widespread that prisons often provided better nutrition and care than was available to the 'deserving poor' outside. There are similar problems in Africa today, where many countries still suffer greatly from economic underdevelopment, and the political oppression, corruption and conflict that both produce and result from poverty.

This is not the whole story, and considerable efforts are being made in some countries to reform prisons despite these challenges.[17] I saw this for myself in Kenya a few years ago, when I visited five prisons, including two women's establishments, to evaluate measure taken to protect human rights, including implementation of the 'Standard Minimum Rules for the Treatment of Prisoners'. This guide to humane treatment was adopted by the UN in 1955 and expanded in 2015 when, in honour of that most famous of political prisoners, it became known as 'the Nelson Mandela Rules'.[18] Prisoners told me that their treatment had improved in recent years, obviously from a low base given that the examples they gave me included the sharp reduction in arbitrary 'beatings' from staff. Nevertheless, the independent Kenyan state, while retaining the system it inherited, has tried to

Figure 3.2: 'Mandela Rules' sign at Shimo La Tewa Women's Prison, Mombasa, Kenya

layer into it a greater ethos of human rights, including access to rehabilitation and education, which was widely available, supported by staff and highly valued by prisoners.

Kenya has also established a probation service, which is unusual in Africa, and implemented non-custodial sentences and early release initiatives to mitigate overcrowding. The effort and commitment of Kenyan officials was clear, but in many respects their work reinforced some of the contradictions about purpose. For example, their attempts to invest in a risk assessment process imported from the West to classify prisoners seemed an odd priority for a system with fundamental problems such as a lack of resources for repairs, overcrowding and some degrading practices (see Chapter 6).

Asserting a place in the world: Japan

In the nineteenth century, many countries cast admiring glances towards the new penitentiaries of the West, which were assumed to be successfully reducing crime through their modern prison regimes. They included independent nations that had avoided colonization, local colonial powers such as Japan, and countries that had thrown off the colonial yoke relatively early; in Latin America, where the Spanish had largely been expelled by 1825, '[public debates] usually pointed to the sharp contrast between what they saw (and were ashamed of) in their own countries and the "successes" of "civilised" nations'.[19]

Drawing inspiration from the American penitentiary and European prison experiments, Japan built its first modern prison in 1874.[20] Daniel V. Botsman's nuanced and detailed work discusses the complex factors that have shaped Japanese punishment; for our purposes, I will pull out three main messages that are important to our understanding of what the prison represents.

First, Botsman describes how new forms of punishment were part of broader social change in nineteenth-century Japan as it sought to harness the energies of its people, while remedying national 'weaknesses', which included criminals and others who might hinder the emergence of a modern and industrious nation: 'in this regard the establishment of a modern criminal justice and penal system was clearly an integral part of the larger process of "nation building"'.[21]

In an echo of Foucault, Botsman argues that the plan for a modern prison system was part of a new vision of disciplinary power, as 'people's lives would now increasingly be shaped by their progress through a series of institutions designed to mold them into modern subject-citizens',[22] with the prison sweeping up all those who 'somehow fell through the disciplinary cracks'.[23]

Second, Japan's efforts to reconceptualize its own position as a rising world power at the end of the nineteenth century led officials to look towards the West rather than China or other parts of Asia for ideas on prison reform. Japanese thinking was substantially influenced by the misleading but influential descriptions by Japanese commentators of American prisons as places of both discipline and successful reform.[24]

Third, the desire to emulate the West in making better use of prison labour to build the nation played a particularly important role in the early development of Japanese capitalism and in turn supported the objectives of prison-builders. This came at enormous human cost: between 1884 and 1894 nearly 44,000 people died in Japanese prisons, mostly as a result of malnutrition, exhaustion, and accidents while working.[25]

When I visited two Japanese prisons in 2015 – Tochigi women's prison and Fuchu men's prison – I felt that I had stepped into the past, so striking were the similarities with what I had read about the early

American penitentiaries. Unlike in Kenya, where prisoners often sat, talked and walked together, there was almost no verbal interaction. I found it particularly disconcerting to walk into a canteen where about a hundred women were having lunch in total silence.

The value ascribed to discipline and mental strength was clear. Two English prisoners in Tochigi said that they did not fear the physical violence that afflicts so many of the world's prisons but experienced 'mental cruelty' as a result of the regime and rules. Unlike Japanese prisoners, foreign women were normally in single cells, which had some advantages but also meant that they were isolated from others. They were not allowed to speak their own languages and, like all prisoners, were normally forbidden to speak at all when they were working. The isolation was compounded by the fact that phone calls were not allowed and visits were behind glass screens. The regime was taking its toll: Tochigi held 670 women at the time of my visit and prison officials told me that a fifth of them had some form of eating disorder and that half experienced mental or physical ill health.

In the men's prison, I saw a lot of prisoners marching from place to place, with guards shouting instructions. Whenever we passed them on the walkways, prisoners were ordered to turn around and look in the other direction, and in the silent workshops no one looked at us as we entered. There were more prisoners than available work – which involved fixing plastic parts to each other – so the men queued in silence until their turn came to work, and were quickly reprimanded if their gaze wavered. One man described Fuchu as 'not a prison but a forced labour camp/mental asylum'. The rigid discipline was illustrated by the punishments for infringement of prison rules; prison officials told us that the maximum punishment was 60 days kneeling in front of a wall for eight hours a day. I wondered if I had misheard when I was told that this punishment had been applied to prisoners who broke the rule against attempting suicide.

There is another reason why Japan is such an intriguing case study: despite a prison system that is very different from the celebrated Nordic model, Japan's reoffending rate is low and the prison population is exceptionally low[26] at 36 per 100,000. This compares with 136 per 100,000 in England and Wales and is significantly lower even than in Europe's least carceral countries, Norway and Finland.[27] The low crime rate can be ascribed to a number of factors, such as Japan being a high conformity society where rule-breaking is severely frowned upon and having an ageing population that is less likely to be involved in crime. But the low rate of imprisonment is also something to do with the way that the Japanese state is able to respond to the problem of offending as a whole through a focus on community involvement in the prevention of crime.[28] For example, Japan makes exceptionally good use of probation volunteers who are 50 times as numerous as Japan's professional probation officers, who support, supervise and train the volunteers.[29]

Building the economy: Russia

Russia's prison system provides an instructive contrast to the countries discussed so far. It evolved under a monarchy, was mobilized during the Soviet era to serve the needs of communism and, following a brief democratic interlude, now exists under an effective autocracy. It was not until Laura Piacentini's seminal study was published in 2004 that Russian prisons started to be better understood outside the country.[30] Piacentini's work describes the development of a Soviet penal system that had little to do with what we would typically think of as crime: 'a Soviet prisoner's crime was judged according to the extent that it "wrecked" Soviet harmony. In this sense, all crime was that which was politically and culturally harmful to Marxist/Leninist ideology'.[31]

The notion of reformation that developed from this starting point was an extreme version of the social and individual rehabilitation ideals that already characterized Western prisons in the early to mid-twentieth century. In the Soviet Union, prisoners were to be politically indoctrinated as they worked, and these two objectives 'formed the basis of a century-long penal identity that aimed for social cohesiveness and the survival of the state through various social control measures'.[32] The work was usually to develop natural resources where wage labour was considered too expensive. Prisoners could be sent anywhere labour was required, often to distant camps known as 'gulags', where hundreds of thousands died during the Stalinist era. The camps were largely self-sufficient and produced surplus income for use by both local and national government. By the 1980s, it was obvious that prison labour was not incidental but central to the maintenance of Soviet political and economic ideology. International prison expert Andrew Coyle summarizes the situation as follows: 'Prisoners in Soviet times were regarded as enemies of the State ... One thing which the State could demand from them in return was labour. This principle was added to the earlier Tsarist system of exile to far-flung parts of the Empire.'[33] Coyle adds that while Soviet administrators may have had a vague expectation that they might change their attitude to society while undertaking the required work, this came a 'far second' to the requirement for economic production.[34]

Millions of prisoners were released following Stalin's death in 1952, but his successors upheld the Soviet principle that prisons were to articulate state power and ideology. It was only when the Soviet Union collapsed in 1991 that its penal identity was finally uncoupled from this philosophy.[35] The numbers in prison remained high but were much reduced in line with the declining importance of industrial production in what were now 15 independent and divergent national penal systems. As Coyle puts it, 'Suddenly the lorry chassis which was built in Ukraine could not be linked up with the cabin which was built in Georgia or with the wheels made in Siberia.'[36]

Russia's prison system today retains powerful echoes of this Soviet past – penal or correctional colonies where prisoners are forced to work are still the norm, and the term 'prison' is generally used to describe only a small number of high-security establishments. There is less purpose to the penal colonies than in the past and a sense of uncertainty about what principles should define the modern Russian penal system. Very poor conditions, corruption, violence and informal rules (rather than the rule of law) persist,[37] and the use of torture is not in dispute: on the infrequent occasions that the Russian authorities have allowed publication of monitoring reports by the European Committee for the Prevention of Torture (CPT), it has documented clear-cut cases of torture, and impunity for state officials,[38] while the Russian press has itself revealed multiple cases of torture and other forms of ill-treatment.[39]

Nation-building

In the twenty-first century, scholars cannot assess prisons as if they derive from, rather than produce, the bounded nation-state. Prisons are places where the meaning of citizenship is crafted ...' (Emma Kaufman and Mary Bosworth)[40]

A purpose of prison that emerges with some force from this examination is its role in defining and building the nation. Whether it is Japan imprisoning its 'weaker elements' to stop them undermining economic development, Russia using prison to politically indoctrinate and economically exploit, or the British intimidating their way into a position of ongoing dominance in colonized Africa, prison has been used, at least in part, to enforce the national vision of the powerful. It has developed in the context of what is still a relatively new world socio-political order: it was only in the mid-seventeenth century that the Treaty of Westphalia asserted the right to national sovereignty and laid the foundations for the global establishment of Western-style nation states.[41] This was followed by the subsequent popular aspiration of independent 'nationhood' and the exponential growth of nations.

Nations were famously portrayed by Benedict Anderson as 'imagined communities',[42] amounting to socially constructed ideas serving political and economic ends. Nation-building is what politicians mean when they talk about unity, national cohesion and the importance of serving the 'ordinary people'. The goal is a fictitious ethnic and cultural homogeneity that can reinforce a national identity and political unity.[43] There is consequently a need for some form of binding force to develop what in many respects is the illusion of nationhood. The criminal justice system can be one such force, generating social solidarity by identifying the 'bad' people and, in so doing, validating the 'good' ones. This points to the social functionality, even desirability, of crime and imprisonment.

If we accept this line of argument, then the idea of the nation today is inevitably challenged by non-conformist behaviours and diverse identities. Immigration, ethnic diversity, and the social and economic development that allows poorer people to become more influential in a society, all subject nationhood to cultural reshaping and constant re-creation, which challenge national identity and fuel social tensions. In the Global North in particular, it becomes ever more important in this context to ask difficult questions about why we see grossly disproportionate imprisonment of both foreign nationals and minority ethnic people.[44]

We may simply assume these groups are inherently more criminal; but a more credible answer is that the nation-building purpose of prison is not merely historical, but an ongoing process. In the West, it manifests through prisons and immigration detention centres being used to manage people who cross borders. What is referred to as the 'criminalization of migration' has seen both the creation and stricter enforcement of criminal offences to regulate migration, and, on a more symbolic level, the use of the language, processes and institutions usually associated with the criminal justice system.[45] Hence, for example, we see the creation of immigration detention centres based on prison designs, and language that emphasizes a loosely defined 'threat' from migrants.[46] The close relationship between nationalism, race, immigration control and the prison is explored in legal scholar Emma Kaufman's book *Punish and Expel* in which she combines theoretical depth and painstaking empirical prison research to conclude that race and nationality should be seen not as secondary features, but rather as 'structural principles of imprisonment',[47] and that people are incarcerated as a result of the 'aftermath of border-focused prison policies'.[48] Kaufman succinctly articulates what we are really talking about when we speak of people detained for immigration purposes in prisons or immigration detention centres: the control and punishment of people who don't fit into an artificial category (citizen).

The prison therefore plays a critical role in helping states to maintain dividing lines on the basis of nationality, often with substantial and hidden human impact. I routinely meet prisoners who grew up in the UK, speak with British accents, and have no familial or cultural connection with the countries to which the state is trying to deport them. In effect, they have no meaningful alternative national identity.

Consider the case of Jayden,[49] a Black Jamaican man in his late 20s who had lived in the UK since early childhood and had no significant links to Jamaica. He had been released after completing a sentence for drugs importation but, after a year and a half back in the community, he was detained in prison under immigration powers pending deportation. Jayden had a long history of mental health problems but had been impressively stable after his original release. He had quickly regained employment, was working hard and providing support to both his mentally ill brother and physically unwell mother. He was not considered by his probation officer to be a danger to the public or to pose a high risk of reoffending, and he had long since completed his retributive punishment. He was, to all intents and purposes, rehabilitated.

In prison, Jayden's mental health had rapidly deteriorated, resulting in multiple and determined attempts to kill himself. When I interviewed him, he was despondent, unable to understand why he was not considered to be part of the nation he saw as home, and why his original imprisonment was not sufficient punishment. His confinement had nothing to do with the usual penological purposes of imprisonment and was motivated solely by the purposes of border control.

Overlapping purposes

This chapter and the previous one show that the prison as a means of incapacitation is a far older idea than the prison as a means of punishment, deterrence or rehabilitation, with the latter purposes emerging only in the eighteenth century before taking a grip on penal imagination. At a time of European imperialism, the modern prison evolved from societies that were searching for new and improved ways of sustaining order and controlling their growing, increasingly politicized and challenging (to the elite) populations. They were later exported around the world, sometimes imposed on other countries during periods of imperial domination, and at other times welcomed by independent countries keen to emulate the progress that the supposedly rehabilitative prison appeared to represent. While the reform ideal was most prominent in the West, the prison's role as a means of political control, income generation and building national coherence was in sharper relief in other countries.

All of these roles continue to overlap and vie for primacy in the world's prison systems today. We get closest to conceptual clarity in countries interested in the prison's function of political control and indoctrination, such as in China's mass imprisonment of Uighur Muslims; or in those rare examples, like Norway, where reducing crime is the clear primary objective (see Chapter 7).

One country stands out as perhaps the world's most striking example of conceptual confusion: confinement in its vast and diverse prison systems is justified by the goals of crime and harm reduction, but the state is routinely accused of using prisons as a means of racialized political oppression. We will now turn our gaze towards the US and the broader phenomenon of mass imprisonment.

4

MASS INCARCERATION, RACE AND CRIME

The United States is home to 5 percent of the world's population, but 25 percent of the world's prisoners. ... We keep more people behind bars than the top 35 European countries combined. ... we have also locked up more and more non-violent drug offenders than ever before for longer than ever before. ... In far too many cases the punishment simply does not fit the crime. (President Barack Obama)[1]

Although prison numbers have increased in many parts of the world,[2] 'mass incarceration' is generally linked to the extremes of the US experience, where prison numbers rose rapidly from the mid-1970s and peaked at over 2.3 million in 2008, before beginning a slow descent to around 1.8 million in 2023.[3] 'Tough on crime' policies were encouraged by public and political consternation at rising crime rates from the mid-1960s into the 1970s, but the sudden growth in numbers was still unexpected. While the prison population in 1975 was around 380,000, it had been going down for almost twenty years and there was even a belief in some quarters that prison would cease to be a common response to social problems.[4] Yet by 2008, the US incarceration rate of 756 per 100,000 of the population was the highest there has ever been in a democratic state, and compares to just 93 per 100,000 in 1972. Moreover, while mass imprisonment had some depressant effect on the crime rate, the connection between the two was far from straightforward, as we shall see, and from the mid-1990s there was in fact no evidence that the relentless rise in incarceration was having any effect on crime at all. Was this just a logical crime-reducing policy that got out of hand or was there more going on?

Penal populism and the 'war on drugs'

Penal populists allow the electoral advantage of a policy to take precedence over its penal effectiveness. In short, penal populism consists of the pursuit of a set of penal policies to win votes rather than to reduce crime rates or to promote justice. (Julian Roberts et al.)[5]

Most examinations of mass incarceration conclude that it resulted from political choices rooted in what has been described as 'popular punitiveness' or 'penal populism'. These terms describe a process whereby politicians compete to look tough on crime and thereby garner the support of what are assumed to be generally punitive electorates. This is most often achieved through more imprisonment regardless of impact on crime rates or long-term societal benefits. Penal populists often claim, as David Garland puts it, to take their lead from 'long-suffering, ill-served people, above all from victims' and defer to the voices of what might be described as 'common sense' or 'what everyone knows'.[6]

Thus the seeds of the US prison explosion were sown by the administration of President Richard Nixon who, in June 1971, announced that drug abuse had 'assumed the dimensions of a national emergency' and that drugs were now 'public enemy number one'.[7] On one level, this was surprising as Nixon had previously advocated

Figure 4.1: Cartoon by Thomas Scott, 21 June 1990, *The Evening Post*, New Zealand

investment in drug treatment and public health, rather than punishment.[8] But at a time of public concern over crime rates that had been increasing over the previous decade, a new strategy was deemed necessary – but it was by no means clear that it had much to do with either drug use or crime. Senior government officials have subsequently confirmed that the Nixon administration exercised penal populism in a calculated fashion to control groups on which it could not rely for votes. For example, John Ehrlichman, a Watergate co-conspirator and Nixon's head of domestic policy, revealed that:

> The Nixon campaign in 1968, and the Nixon White House after that, had two enemies: the antiwar left and black people. You understand what I'm saying? We knew we couldn't make it illegal to be either against the war or black, but by getting the public to associate the hippies with marijuana and blacks with heroin, and then criminalizing both heavily, we could disrupt those communities. We could arrest their leaders, raid their homes, break up their meetings, and vilify them night after night on the evening news. Did we know we were lying about the drugs? Of course we did.[9]

Similarly, Nixon aide H.R. Haldeman reported that Nixon 'emphasized that you have to face the fact that the *whole* problem is really the blacks. The key is to devise a system that recognizes this while appearing not to.'[10]

This willingness to stoke and exploit concern about drugs for political gain was escalated dramatically during the presidency of Ronald Reagan, whose version of the war on drugs – at a time, it should be noted, when drug use had been *falling* for a few years – contributed to a doubling of the prison population. In 1986, the Anti-Drug Abuse Act imposed mandatory minimums for drug offences, including a five-year mandatory minimum for the simple possession or sale of five grams of crack cocaine – a drug used primarily by Black people. In contrast, the mandatory minimum trigger for powder cocaine, a chemically identical drug to crack – but used primarily by white people – required the sale of *100 times that amount*. Before the enactment of the Anti-Drug Abuse Act, the average federal drug sentence for Black people was 11 per cent higher than for white people. Four years later, that figure had increased to 49 per cent.[11]

The 'war on drugs' continued, supported by the 'tough on crime' policies of Presidents Bush and Clinton and, by 1997, drug offences accounted for a fifth of state prisoners and nearly two thirds of federal prisoners.[12] It was not until the US Congress passed the Fair Sentencing Act in 2010 that imprisonment of drug offenders, many of whom were serving long sentences for possession alone, started to reduce. In particular, this Act reduced the disparity between crack cocaine and pure cocaine from 100–1 to 18–1.[13] Barack Obama's election seems to have helped galvanize a growing consensus that continuing mass incarceration was not a tenable response to either crime or the fear of crime. While there is 'growing evidence that the overreliance on incarceration has reached a turning point',[14] the pace of decline is glacial. The average drop of 2.3 per cent annually means that it would take until 2098 to return to 1972's prison population,[15] although the Biden administration's recent decriminalization of cannabis may well increase the speed of decline.[16]

A final point to make on penal populism is that it is a strategy built on shaky foundations. Policy makers routinely over-estimate the punitiveness of the public, and the public generally thinks that crime is far more prevalent and serious than it really is.[17] While many people still see sentencing as too lenient, when they are given the details of individual cases and the human stories behind the crimes, they are much less punitive.[18] This knowledge is useful to bear in mind when we discuss possible futures for the prison in Chapter 7.

Race and mass incarceration

Large racial disparities in incarceration focused any negative effects of incarceration disproportionately on African Americans, the poor in particular, and transformed their collective relationship to the state. (National Research Council)[19]

Demonization is penal populism's weapon of choice: demonization of communities, offenders in general and Black offenders in particular, and perhaps also of opponents of harsh measures who may, for example, be labelled 'liberal apologists' making us unsafe by being soft on criminals. Demonization creates and thrives on fear, and is arguably a way of constructing a justification for state negligence (because 'the bad/ scary guys don't *deserve* our help').

A particularly infamous illustration of this process – which led directly to an acceleration of both mass incarceration and to the rise in Black people being caught up in it – is the advert that Republican presidential candidate George Bush ran against his Democratic party opponent, Mike Dukakis, during the 1988 election campaign.[20] A Black man, Willie Horton, had been serving a life sentence for murder when he committed further serious offences during a short furlough (an unsupervised temporary release), intended to support his reintegration into society. The furlough programme was not particularly controversial, and was widely supported not just by Dukakis but by many Republicans. The risks were generally considered justified when weighed against the benefits and there were few failures. Yet Bush's advert, featuring a 'very scary looking, dishevelled, wild-eyed black man',[21] successfully implied that Dukakis would be responsible for more 'scary' Blacks like Willie Horton being on the streets, feeding deep fears rooted in racism. Subsequently, no politician was willing to be seen as anything other than 'tough on crime', and debate about progressive criminal justice reforms was effectively stifled for several decades.

As will be clear by now, sooner or later, virtually every analysis of mass incarceration in the US alights on the issue of race. The over-representation of Black people in prisons or under other forms of state control emerged more or less when the American Civil War ended in 1865 and resulted directly from a combination of white people's anxiety about freed Black people, fear of crime, and the loss of free Black labour at a time of economic depression.[22] But it was not until the 1980s that the consistent racial disproportionality in US prisons exploded. Since then, the hunger for imprisonment in the US has been satisfied by the grossly disproportionate confinement of Black Americans; they comprised 13 per cent of the US population but 38 per cent of its prisoners in 2019.[23] Black Americans are five times more likely to be in prison than white people[24] and the experience often reverberates throughout their lives, families and communities (see Chapter 5). Criminal records can lead to what is sometimes referred to as a 'social death'[25] as a result of, for example, loss of food stamps and public assistance, loss of voting rights and restrictions on employment and even driving licences in some states.

This approach reflects neoliberal values of personal responsibility and the rational choice theory of crime, which emphasizes individual agency and considered decision-making processes in the commission of offences (see Chapter 5). At its simplest, rational choice theory postulates that when the costs of punishment outweigh the gains of crime, the offender will choose to do something else instead. Structural explanations for offending behaviour, including class, poverty, social context and discrimination, are given little credence. At its worst, the theory pathologizes Black people as inherently criminal – otherwise, the argument goes, why would so many be in prison? Michelle Alexander's structural analysis of race and incarceration in the US is not the first,[26] but has become the most celebrated challenge to this perspective: 'It is fair to say that we have witnessed an evolution in the United States from a racial caste system based entirely on exploitation (slavery), to one based largely on subordination (Jim Crow), to one defined by marginalization (mass incarceration).'[27]

Alexander views mass incarceration as a comprehensive system of racialized social control, which resonates strongly with the system of legally enforced discrimination in the US, known as the 'Jim Crow' laws. There is indeed a profound symbolism of former slave plantations being repurposed as prisons and disproportionately filled with Black people. A famous example is Louisiana State Penitentiary, a vast maximum security prison which is still commonly referred to as 'Angola', a name it acquired to reflect the national origin of many of the slaves who were forced to work on the plantation. Albert Woodfox, who spent more than four decades in solitary confinement at Angola, writes about his early experiences there:

> The horrors of the prison in 1965 cannot be exaggerated ... The prisoner population was segregated; most prisoners were black. African American prisoners did 99 percent of the fieldwork by hand, usually without gloves or proper footwear. White guards on horseback rode up and down the lines of working prisoners, holding shotguns across their laps and constantly yelling at the men who were working, saying, 'Work faster, old thing' or, 'N****r.'[28]

It is remarkable that the high rate of Black American incarceration today is nevertheless a significantly improved picture. The decrease in the US prison population since 2008 has been steeper for Black people compared with other ethnicities, amounting to a 34 per cent drop between 2006 and 2018.[29] This lends further support to the view that many did not need to be there in the first place.

The racism in American criminal justice is not difficult to pin down given the fairly direct lines that can be drawn between slavery and imprisonment. But this pattern is also visible in other countries, including England and Wales, one of the most ethnically diverse countries of Europe and among its most prolific incarcerators. The first thing to note is that while total numbers incarcerated in England and Wales are lower than in the US, which may make the problem seem less acute, relative to their representation in the population the number of prisoners identifying as Black is proportionately *higher*. In a process that is not dissimilar to the effect of the Jim Crow laws in the US, when Britain and other European countries abolished outright slavery, they replaced it with indentured labour or debt bondage. This meant that the poor, usually male, labourer was tied to his employer for the duration of sometimes lengthy contracts, often in poor conditions and for low wages. Up to two million people from the Asian sub-continent and Africa were sent to different parts of European colonies to work on plantations and other colonial industries as indentured labourers after the end of formal slavery.[30] This system

WHAT ARE PRISONS FOR?

only ended between the First World War and the middle of the twentieth century, and many of those who had come as labourers stayed in Europe, arguably becoming prime targets for new forms of control through the criminal justice system.

There is, in short, more resonance for Europeans in the US experience than is usually assumed, and while the US experience is compelling, it should not be seen as wholly exceptional.

What effect did mass incarceration have on crime?

Many of the things that governments have done to reduce crime rates in recent decades have been largely epiphenomenal – normatively and politically important, and having major effects on many people's lives, but pretty much beside the point in terms of crime rates and patterns. (Michael Tonry)[31]

Researchers have struggled to come up with consistent estimates, but a rigorous evaluation by the US National Research Council concluded that increased incarceration 'may have caused a decrease in crime, but the magnitude is highly uncertain and the results of most studies suggest it was unlikely to have been large'.[32] The Vera Institute of Justice similarly concluded that increases in US incarceration rates had only a small impact on crime rates at best, while 'somewhere between 75 and 100 percent of the reduction in crime rates since the 1990s is explained by other factors'.[33] These factors included an ageing population, higher wages, more employment, more law enforcement personnel and changes in policing strategies. Furthermore, any crime reduction benefits of incarceration were limited to property crime rather than violent crime, while in some areas with high incarceration rates, there seemed to be a tipping point beyond which increased use of imprisonment became an indicator of a *higher* crime rate; this was partly because of the 'university of crime' thesis, whereby prison is a place for people to learn criminal habits and make criminal associations,[34] and partly because of the anti-social behaviour that is more likely to occur following loss of employment, housing and family ties. Natasha Frost and Todd Clear, carefully avoiding any hint of overstatement, summarize the overwhelming conclusion of repeated research as follows: 'although few would argue that crime and incarceration are entirely disconnected, many have demonstrated that the connection is tenuous and that the relationship between changing rates of incarceration and fluctuating rates of crime is at best imperfect'.[35]

One reason that the ultimate crime-reducing effect of mass incarceration is so hard to identify is that its impact on offending is brought into question as soon as we look beyond the temporary effect of incapacitation. Todd Clear's work demonstrates the long-term damage of mass incarceration to family and community ties, health and social capability, including ability to obtain work and accommodation, all factors that are ultimately associated with higher crime. Clear also shows that US mass imprisonment removed emotional and financial support from prisoners' families and communities, creating instability and resentment towards the state, and making it more likely that children would fall into crime.[36] A recent study shows that nearly half (45 per cent) of all American adults have had an immediate family member incarcerated and partners left at home are disproportionately likely to experience health and financial problems, and homelessness.[37]

There is similarly strong evidence of the insubstantiality of the link between crime rates and prison in the UK, where the House of Commons Justice Committee pointed out more than a decade ago[38] that it is virtually impossible to find a causal link between the use of prison and a fall in crime rates. The Committee cited the comparison between the US and Europe, which had both shown a marked fall in crime rates while pursuing divergent incarceration policies, and pointed out that crime rates had dropped *more slowly* in England and Wales than in the rest of Europe despite relatively *higher* rates of imprisonment. In short, the tenuous link between crime reduction and imprisonment suggests that the former cannot be the main purpose of the latter.

Can mass incarceration increase crime?

Away from the US, we find intriguing evidence of the *crime-increasing* effects of mass incarceration. South America is well known to have huge problems with gangs, drugs and crime, and has tried to manage them through more use of imprisonment. Brazil is a particularly instructive case study: the failure of the Brazilian state to provide basic security and essential services to prisoners birthed a powerful criminal organization that now transcends the prison walls and spills over national borders. The 'Primeiro Comando da Capital' (PCC) originated from prisoners banding together to protect themselves against the arbitrariness and brutality of prison staff, and to find ways to improve prisoners' material conditions.[39] The PCC now has many thousands of members inside and outside Brazilian prisons, with an involvement in the illegal drug trade and violent acquisitive crime that has a reach extending across South America. As one commentator has put it: 'Born in prison, the PCC is an organization immune to prisons. Its top leaders are already behind bars, yet they do not stop operating.'[40]

The perversity of the situation is brought home by Dal Santo's analysis, in which he points out that mass incarceration has actually led to *improvements* in the very poor material conditions that have always characterized Brazilian prisons. While Dal Santo is careful to avoid romanticizing the influence of the PCC, which has achieved and maintained its hegemony through violence, he shows how it has encouraged a productive spirit of cooperation among prisoners. For example, the PCC promotes conflict resolution, forbids the use of weapons and has eliminated crack cocaine use,[41] while helping prisoners with basic needs such as hygiene kits when they arrive in prison and bus fares when they leave.[42] If we return to one of the key official purposes of prison, incapacitation to contain and prevent criminality, it is clear that the opposite has happened in Brazil. The depiction of people in prison as irredeemably bad or uncaring is also challenged by such evidence. On the contrary, this seems to be an impressive example of cooperation and mutual support fuelled by the same sense of abandonment and injustice that contributes to criminality in the community.

Changing the narrative of mass imprisonment

A striking contrast to the US and the UK is Finland's decision in the 1950s to pursue a long-term decarceration policy at a time when its prison population was four times higher than in other Nordic countries and among the highest in Europe. Finland's incarcerated population fell to the same level as in other Nordic countries at the beginning of the 1990s, and by 2023 it was substantially below that of both Sweden and Denmark, and just below the rate in Norway. Finland now has one of the world's lowest rates of imprisonment and there has been no rise in crime rates.[43] How did this happen? First of all, there was, as Patrik Törnudd put it: 'an almost unanimous conviction that Finland's internationally high prisoner rate was a disgrace and that it would be possible to significantly reduce the amount and length of prison sentences without serious repercussions on the crime situation'.[44]

A critical factor was the consensus among political parties and state officials that a new direction in penal policy was needed. Another criminologist, Tapio Lappi-Seppälä, sets out further reasons why change was possible: he describes an 'exceptionally expert-oriented' criminal justice policy (in contrast to penal populism's denigration of expertise); a readiness among the judiciary to support decarceration; an absence of political opposition to reform and, at least until the early 1990s, a Finnish media that declined to sensationalize penal policy concerns, preferring a 'sober and reasonable attitude towards issues of criminal policy'.[45] The effect was a 'normalization' of prison rates 'from a level that was totally absurd to a level that can be considered to be a fair Nordic level'.[46] More broadly, not just prison but the idea of punishment itself came to be regarded as just 'one option among many' crime control strategies, which were now much more explicitly seen to include social development policy, environmental planning and situational crime prevention.[47]

The list of factors that supported decarceration in Finland may at first glance look like a distant dream in most Western countries. It is often argued that the Nordic countries have many features which distinguish them even from other European nations, including relatively wealthy and welfare-orientated societies where penal populism is largely in check. But while critical thinking is sensible, fatalism and lack of ambition is not: Lappi-Seppälä points out that Finland experienced severe social and structural change as it moved from a rural economy to an industrial urban welfare state, which resulted in steep increases in recorded crime rates from the mid-1960s to the mid-1970s (reflecting the timescale of rising US crime rates), and again during the 1980s. But this did not stall the decline in prison numbers. It is also worth stressing that at no point did the fall in imprisonment have a discernible impact on crime rates. It would therefore be myopic, to put it mildly, to ignore the lessons and the vision that such societies offer, even if we think that our own national contexts are currently very different.

A key message from the Finnish and contrasting US examples is that political leadership is immensely important to the direction of penal policy. The point is brought home by the experience of the UK in the decades before the Second World War. Criminologist David Wilson points out that England and Wales experienced one of the world's longest-ever sustained periods of prison population decline between 1908 and the outbreak of the Second World War – from 22,029 to 11,086 (63 to 30 people per 100,000) – and closed about twenty prisons, despite the crime rate in this period actually increasing by around 160 per cent.[48] There are always many factors that lead to such outcomes, but in this case Wilson argues that the tone set by then Home Secretary Winston Churchill was potentially decisive. Churchill pointed out that about two thirds of sentenced prisoners in 1910 were incarcerated for two weeks or less, 'a terrible and purposeless waste of public money and human character', and set about reducing the prison population. Leadership is more effective when it seeks fertile ground, and Wilson identifies other important factors, including scepticism over what prison could achieve; a belief that the newly formed probation service could offer viable alternatives; and a belief among politicians and key social groups that prison was a counterproductive experience. In any event, Churchill's leadership may well have been the critical galvanizing factor that led to change, in the same way that Finland's leaders chose the right conditions for the reforms that took place there.

An obvious solution?

The US has combined the economic and social control functions of prison that we saw in Chapter 3 with greater enthusiasm than most. So established is the network of private and public interests that have supported the growth of the US prison system, that it has been given a distinct label, popularized by abolitionist Angela Davis: 'Because of the extent to which prison building and operation began to attract vast amounts of capital – from the construction industry to food and health care provision – in a way that recalled the emergence of the military industrial complex, we began to refer to a "prison industrial complex".'

This 'prison industrial complex' has helped to embed prison as a solution to economic, social and political problems, and is arguably the main reason that reversing course towards decarceration has been so slow. In the meantime, there is no doubt that mass incarceration has already exacted a substantial and racialized toll on human potential and self-fulfilment, while appearing to fail any reasonable social or economic cost–benefit test. The problem of mass incarceration is not just defined through numbers and racial injustice in the US, but in its normalization of a fundamentally abnormal state of affairs. Its insistent message is that prison is the obvious solution to crime and the only means of delivering a meaningful punishment. Finland remains one of a select group of countries that have successfully disrupted this equation. In most countries, it takes a considerable effort of the imagination to see an alternative to prison or to see as individuals the people who comprise the massed ranks of prisoners. The next two chapters will now try to address these problems by delving deeper into the details of prison life and the stories of prisoners and their families.

5

DO THE CRIME, DO THE TIME? WHO ARE PRISONERS?

If only it were all so simple! If only there were evil
people somewhere insidiously committing evil deeds,
and it were necessary only to separate them from the
rest of us and destroy them. But the line dividing good
and evil cuts through the heart of every human being.
(Aleksandr Solzhenitsyn)[1]

Up to now, we have been considering the purposes of
prisons by exploring broad histories and theories that
cut across geographical and temporal barriers. But it
is only by understanding more about people in prison
and putting a human face to the history and theory that
we can start to build a more detailed appreciation of
what the prison is, or is not, achieving. In this chapter, I
will therefore try to ground thinking about the prison's
deterrent, retributive and rehabilitative purposes

by exploring common social and psychological characteristics of prisoners. I will also try to give some insight into life in prisons disproportionately filled with unwell, disadvantaged and neurodiverse people in this chapter and the next. We must then consider how far common prison objectives still make sense in light of that knowledge.

Making choices to offend

Karen's story

I knew Karen for about two years when I worked in a community probation office. She was a white woman in her early thirties whose attendance at probation appointments was at best erratic. She had been in and out of prison many times, serving short sentences after breaching community orders and for offences such as shoplifting, threatening behaviour and resisting arrest. Conversations with her were usually difficult. She had been diagnosed with a personality disorder, often lied or exaggerated, was regularly intoxicated, flirted with male officers and was quick to take offence when seen by women probation officers.

Like many people in prison, Karen was also a victim of crime. She had been raped and subjected to other violent crimes, often perpetrated when she was trying to obtain drugs or alcohol, was engaged in sex work or was simply at home with her abusive partner. She had a child who was in the care of the local authority. Karen had a network of professionals around her to support, supervise and control her. It would be fair to say that most of these workers were sympathetic but exasperated at the range of problems that she presented and the fact that she seemed unable to make changes. She was set in her lifestyle, and no amount of talking, threatening or persuading seemed to make a difference. Prison was seen by most of those concerned, including some of her sentencers, as ineffectual, but they could not think what else to do.

I am not sure, within the current system, what would have stopped Karen from committing what were generally considered minor offences or helped her to avoid the persistent victimization that marked her life. But I am sure that prison was achieving none of its stated purposes with her – it was a desperate last move, grounded in the hope that at some point she would make a rational choice to desist and that the prospect of more punishment would, eventually, be enough to deter her.

You may feel that too many excuses are made for people like Karen and that, in the words of former UK prime minister John Major, 'society needs to condemn a little more and understand a little less'.[2] The conservative polemicist Peter Hitchens is a more recent and strident proponent of this position.[3] At the heart of much of his writing is the image of the calculating and faceless criminal who deserves swift and long prison sentences or, in the most serious of cases, death. Criminals are, with few exceptions, portrayed as chancers and rogues, sometimes monsters. They are entirely culpable for the decisions that lead them to imprisonment, and sympathy should be reserved exclusively for the victims of crime.

Readers may sympathize with the focus on individual culpability, if not the polemics, in this argument. It is a position that elevates what is known as the 'rational choice theory' of crime, an approach that governments generally rely on when making policy to reduce crime. In brief, the theory proposes that people who commit crimes do so having weighed up the costs, benefits and available opportunities. It encourages a focus on deterring crime, partly by making the costs too high – for example, with longer sentences and harsher regimes – as well as by reducing opportunities for crime through tactics such as installing window locks, street lighting or CCTV. The theory does not quite go so far as saying that people always make a calculated choice to engage in crime and have an equal opportunity to make a different choice, but it encourages that position. It has little interest in how unique backgrounds or social disadvantages may influence an individual's criminal behaviour, or the subsequent role of the prison in preventing future crime, encouraging us instead to focus on individual decision-making. In this view, crime reduction is to be achieved through retribution and deterrent punishment.

While the practical crime prevention measures it promotes (known as 'situational' crime prevention) have been effective in reducing some types of offences, rational choice theory tends towards a reductionist logic which underplays the impact on a person's decision-making of social context, personal history and psychological make-up. It assumes we all have the same opportunity to make prosocial choices. If that were true, we would expect prisoners to represent a rough cross-section of society. Instead, we see, for example, that they are far more likely than others in their community to experience poverty, low education status, illiteracy, unemployment, low income, mental health problems, drug misuse, violence, trauma and abuse.[4]

There are, of course, people who choose to offend despite good health, personal capacity, social capital (a network of positive relationships) and opportunities that make good decisions easier to take. But continuing to commit crime, and taking the stress, disapproval and rejection that comes with it, is not an easy lifestyle choice. So it stands to reason that there are few persistent offenders who have coolly weighed up the pros and cons of their behaviours and still make the choice to break the law.

How is poverty linked to imprisonment?

[I]ndividuals enter prisons with various disadvantages and sometimes return to their communities with even more, not to mention that the communities themselves are often characterized by high levels of social and economic disadvantage. (Daniel P. Mears and Joshua C. Cochran)[5]

While the least powerful and most disadvantaged people in society are more likely to be in prison, it would be an extreme and insulting simplification to suggest that poverty leads to crime. Most people in all income groups are largely law-abiding, and the fact that crime is continuing to fall despite recessions in Western economics indicates that there is not a neat link with poverty, unemployment and other aspects of a depressed economy.

But poverty undoubtedly creates individual and social vulnerabilities that increase the risk of people ending up in prison. A person's position in the social hierarchy is tied to the chances of them being drawn into the criminal justice system, partly because those with more social power, for example corporate criminals, are less likely to be caught or convicted of offences, let alone imprisoned. It is also the case that families with relatively more wealth are more likely to provide support mechanisms that can prevent an uninterrupted slide into, for example, crime associated with gambling, alcohol or drug misuse, and fund realistic treatment options.

The prison's function of disciplining the poor comes into sharp relief in countries of the Global South, where absolute poverty is more prevalent than in the Global North. For example, in Sri Lanka, the vast majority of people have committed offences associated with poverty or mental ill health and, in 2020, 74 per cent of prisoners were incarcerated because they could not pay their fines.[6] We also see direct penalization of poverty in Africa where, despite efforts at reform, most countries still criminalize those who are 'idle' or experience homelessness. In many African countries, the penalty for 'vagrancy' ranges from six months to two years, while begging can lead to up to seven years' imprisonment.[7]

But explicit criminalization of poverty is not confined to poorer countries. In England and Wales, as in all Western countries, people rarely end up in prison until they have committed multiple or serious offences, but human rights lawyer Rona Epstein's research discovered that people who have committed no criminal offence at all are still being given sentences of between 12 and 52 weeks, typically because they break injunctions relating to begging, sleeping rough, shouting or other forms of anti-social behaviour.[8] Epstein finds that in the majority of cases, mental ill health is the main cause of the offending, and points out that in France and Norway such behaviours are more likely to trigger a welfare intervention than a punitive one. It is also worth remembering that England's 200-year-old Vagrancy Act, which led to thousands of people being prosecuted and fined every year,[9] often for simply being homeless, was only repealed in 2022.[10]

Mental ill health in prison

> They mostly appear to be either severely mentally ill, off their heads on drugs, or both ... Nothing in my life has prepared me for this moment. (Chris Atkins, author and ex-prisoner)[11]

> I was a schizophrenic and high risk ... sharing a cell with another schizophrenic who was high risk. (Anonymous prisoner)[12]

Prisoners experience a disproportionate rate of psychiatric disorders compared with those in the community, either arriving with conditions that deteriorate in prison or developing a disorder during their imprisonment.[13] The extent of the problem is obscured by the fact that data are easily available only in higher income countries[14] and because what is included under the label of mental illness or disorder varies. But any way that we look at it, the level of mental ill health in prisons is colossal and treatment needs are often unmet. In the US, 44 per cent of those in state prisons and 43 per cent in local jails have a diagnosed mental disorder,[15] and a national survey of mental health needs found that the number of severely mentally ill people in prison was ten times higher than in state psychiatric hospitals.[16]

In the UK, the National Audit Office has concluded that the government does not know how many prisoners have a mental illness, how much it is spending on mental health in prisons or whether it is achieving its objectives.[17] A study across 13 prisons is one of many confirming an exceptionally high incidence of often co-existent health conditions, including personality disorder (experienced by over half of all prisoners, 4.5 times more prevalent than in the community), post-traumatic stress disorder (PTSD) (16 per cent of prisoners, eight times more than in the community) and eating disorders (19.6 per cent – women had a rate 2.5 times higher than in the community, while for men the rate was only slightly higher).[18] Identification and treatment of need is often inadequate, including for those with the most acute psychiatric conditions,[19] and matters are further complicated by the co-existence of multiple problems such as mental illness, drug use and learning disability.

Invisibility

> [P]risons do not disappear problems, they disappear human beings ... in order to convey the illusion of solving social problems. (Angela Davis)[20]

People can be 'lost' in the system because their complex needs and vulnerabilities do not fall easily within diagnostic categories. During a particularly difficult prison inspection, one of my colleagues was asked to talk to a man by other prisoners who were worried about him. Later that day, she walked into the inspectors' meeting room, still visibly angry, and asked me to visit him. I knocked on his cell door and, as usual, waited a while before opening the metal flap covering the small cell window and waving a greeting. One of the reasons that it is useful to look briefly inside a cell before entering is to make sure the person is ready to receive you and isn't, for example, on the toilet. This man lay motionless on his bed (the only furniture I could see) without looking up. As I unlocked his cell door, I was hit by the smell of faeces, body odour and half eaten food. The cell was damp, with a leaking sink and filthy toilet. The man briefly answered any questions I asked but was not focused or 'present' and seemed mentally unwell. If he had seen mental health professionals he was not aware of it. He had been in these conditions for several weeks and staff who, on the whole, were friendly and decent had ceased to notice him. This man possessed a problematic combination for anyone wanting to survive in an overcrowded prison: vulnerability and a lack of disruptive behaviour. He was quiet, caused no problems to staff, and his mental ill health and lack of self-care just didn't register highly enough in the general chaos of prison life.

Such invisibility also contributes, along with the high prevalence of psychosis, depression, personality disorder and substance misuse, to an increased the risk of suicide (see Chapter 6). A major study encompassing 24 high-income countries showed that suicide among women prisoners was typically more than ten times higher than in the general population, and for male prisoners it was three to eight times higher.[21] Suicides following release can be even higher: in England and Wales: men are eight times and women 36 times more likely than their counterparts in the general population to die by suicide within one year of release from prison, a rate similar to that among discharged psychiatric patients.[22]

Trauma

Trauma occurs when people go through very stressful or distressing situations, such as violence, abuse or racism, which cause harmful and long-lasting psychological effects that are difficult to cope with.[23]

The evidence of childhood trauma among prisoners is overwhelming. For example, a Canadian meta-analysis that reviewed 29 studies concluded that half of all Canadian prisoners had experienced physical, sexual or emotional abuse as children.[24] In England and Wales, results are very similar: 53 per cent of women and 27 per cent of men have experienced childhood abuse, compared to 20 per cent in the general population; 50 per cent of women and 40 per cent of men observed violence in the home as children compared to 14 per cent of the general population; and 31 per cent of women and 24 per cent of men were taken into care as children compared to 2 per cent of the general population.[25]

Women are particularly over-represented among those who have been sexually abused (50 per cent of women and 22 per cent of men have experienced sexual abuse) and it is now well established that, much like Karen, imprisoned women tend to have extensive histories of psychological and physical trauma as both adults and children.[26] Many women in prison find the lack of power and control over their lives to be particularly triggering of past trauma, given their histories of intimate partner violence and abuse when others had power over them and misused it.[27]

The prevalence of trauma in prison populations helps to explain very high levels of mental disorder and self-medicating alcohol and drug misuse, which in turn drive reckless and anti-social behaviour and crime, and contribute to high suicide rates. Prisons in England and Wales have started to recognize the implications of such research and there has been a rise in the concept of 'trauma-informed' services, based on the work of American psychologist Stephanie Covington.[28] Staff are trained to understand and take account of the effects of the violent and traumatic histories of people in their care so that they can support the person's recovery and, importantly, avoid inadvertent re-traumatization. While anything that makes staff more aware of prisoners' needs is positive, the evidence for prisons successfully mitigating trauma remains thin,[29] while there is rather more certainty that they certainly produce it (see Chapter 6).

Neurodiversity and traumatic brain injury in prisons

The UK and, to a lesser extent, other parts of Europe, North America and Australia are currently the major sources of research on neurodiversity and criminal justice. Neurodiverse people may be more sensitive to noise, bright artificial lighting and unexpected smells, all of which are in abundance in most prisons. The fact that they may also find it hard to understand and respond quickly to instructions is a dangerous deficit in a place where non-compliance may well be interpreted as threat. They are also more likely to be victimized by other prisoners and to self-harm.[30]

In England and Wales, a comprehensive review of evidence concluded that about half of the adult prison population (a 'conservative' estimate) 'experienced some kind of neurodivergence challenge'[31] compared with 15–20 per cent of the general population. More specifically, while warning that the data are not clear or consistent, the review's authors cautiously offer the following estimates:

- autistic spectrum conditions around three times as prevalent as in the community;
- around a quarter of prisoners with attention deficit hyperactivity disorder;
- 36 per cent of men and 39 per cent of women with a learning disability;
- over half of adult prisoners with dyslexia;
- 80 per cent of prisoners with some kind of speech, language or communication need.

The practical implications of such findings are inadequately understood and this applies even more acutely to the well-hidden condition of traumatic brain injury (TBI), the scale and potentially far-reaching consequences of which rarely fail to shock.

'Traumatic brain injury (TBI) is a "silent epidemic" among people in contact with the law … It has been consistently linked with earlier, more frequent, and more violent offending, and is a barrier to engagement with rehabilitation.'[32] TBI occurs as a result of a blow to the head which causes the brain to move in the skull, and can lead to bruising, bleeding and swelling of the soft brain tissue. The frontal lobes responsible for functions including planning, memory, social skills and emotion regulation are affected, as they sit at the front of the skull. Those affected by TBI are often vulnerable to substance misuse, as they have poorer judgement of the consequences of actions, and higher levels of sensation- or thrill-seeking. Those who misuse substances are also at high risk of TBI due to falls, fights and antisocial behaviour. In summary, TBI makes it more likely that a person will be aggressive and violent, go to prison at a younger age, reoffend, experience homelessness, develop mental health problems, self-harm and have impaired ability to learn, even years after the injury has occurred.[33]

TBI can also be linked to behaviours which are not directly criminal, but can escalate over time. For example, problems with social isolation, poor engagement with education or work, and problems with close personal or family relationships can create barriers for successful living (or reintegration) in society. TBI causes memory and communication problems, and a person with TBI may seem not to be listening, to be uninterested, defiant or obstinate.[34]

In the US, the Centers for Disease Control and Prevention reported that different research studies showed that 25–87 per cent of prisoners reported having experienced a head injury or TBI compared with 8.5 per cent in the general population reporting a TBI.[35] In England and Wales, a cautious estimate is that around half the prison population has suffered a TBI, and around a quarter are likely to experience significant ongoing problems.[36] Research on brain injury in women shows similar prevalence to men, but for women TBI is strongly linked with being assaulted by partners or relatives at home. One study found that 78 per cent of women prisoners had experienced a significant TBI and 40 per cent had an associated disability – domestic violence was the cause of 89 per cent of those injuries.[37]

In ground-breaking UK research in 2015, The Disabilities Trust (known as 'Brainkind' since September 2023) found that TBI is unidentified or routinely misdiagnosed in English and Welsh prisons.[38] The Trust subsequently initiated support services in a few prisons to screen for brain injury and develop tailored support, including for women,[39] with excellent outcomes reported.[40] But such services remain rare and the evidence suggests that we are routinely locking up people with serious, unrecognized and therefore untreated health conditions, which have a direct impact on their behaviour.

Implications

What does all this mean for the purposes of prison? First, it should make us question ideas about deterrence. In theory, severe sentencing and high rates of imprisonment are meant to lead to lower rates of crime because of the deterrent impact on the public (known in criminological theory as 'general deterrence') or the impact on the offender ('specific deterrence'). There is in fact little evidence that prison deters people from offending,[41] let alone if they have some form of mental disorder or neurodiversity. By contrast, there is plentiful evidence that the prospect of being caught by the police, whether real or perceived, has a strong deterrent effect.[42] As penal campaigner and former Chief Inspector of Prisons in England and Wales David Ramsbotham somewhat scathingly commented: 'Deterrence is more of a pious hope in the minds of those who live reasonably pleasant day-to-day lives than a practical reality. Fear of imprisonment may deter those who have a job, a home and a family, but not those who have no hope of achieving or retaining them.'[43]

Second, it should inform our ideas about retribution. Prisons hold disproportionately high numbers of disadvantaged, ill and vulnerable people – like the man my colleague found in his cell surrounded by filth – to which a solely punitive response seems unjust.

Third, and related to this point, it exposes the complexity of rehabilitation – rehabilitative services must creatively and persistently engage people who find it difficult to use them. Providing a service is not the same as ensuring access to it. Like Karen, prisoners across the world are much more likely than people in the general population to have a multitude of social and psychological problems that affect decision-making and ability to engage with services. Criminologist Fergus McNeill has explored the concept of rehabilitation at length:

> in unequal and unjust societies, social conditions may differentially propel some people towards crime and differentially select some for criminalisation. Others are endowed with and propelled towards privilege and unearned social advantages. These criminogenic social

> conditions create obligations on the unjust state and the
> unjust community to repair harms done to the 'offender'.[44]

What McNeill concisely articulates is a responsibility for crime that goes well beyond ascribing it to an individual's personal choice, although it is *not* an argument for absolving them of responsibility. Instead, it is a plea to take a smart and wide-ranging approach to crime by recognizing the multiple causes that give us the prison populations that we have, which include personal choice, social inequality, ill health and structural disadvantage:

> what 'correctional' agencies need to work to correct is not
> an errant individual, but – more often – a broken set of
> social relationships. If offending breaks relationships and
> tears at the social fabric, then *both* the tear *and* the repair
> must be relational; between the people directly involved;
> and between citizen, civil society and state.[45]

This approach resists placing the entire responsibility for offending at the feet of the offender, and accepts that, in an unequal society, we are all implicated in the circumstances that create crime and all have an obligation to help people to desist. McNeill suggests that once the punishment is over and the debt is paid, retributive harms should cease. That means the public actively receiving and supporting released prisoners, who must be able to reintegrate.

I hope that this chapter can help us to move away from a polemicized public debate about punishment, which pits a purist rational choice model that sees prisoners as decontextualized bad people against a structural model that sees them as mere victims. The next chapter will continue to challenge these paradigms by delving further into the lives of people in prison.

6

EXPERIENCING PRISON

Prisons compress lives and emotions into a small space. Conversations from one end of a wing to the other can veer between despair, anger, resignation, relief and hope. I am often emotionally exhausted by the end of a day in prison, but for the prisoners and staff who are there all the time, it is far worse.[1] This chapter will build on Chapter 5 by looking more closely, and rather selectively, at the operation and emotional world of prisons, using prisoner accounts and case studies to give insights into the prison's human impact and purpose. These stories are not intended to supply profound conclusions but to stimulate thought about the lives of people in prison and perhaps to unsettle previous assumptions.

Arriving in prison: fear and anxiety

I finally nodded off, only to be woken an hour later with someone kicking their cell door in. It frightened the life out

of me as I sat up startled. The screams that accompanied
it were like a sound effect you'd use on Halloween; blood
curdling, like someone was being murdered. The sound
of quick footsteps followed by the noise of jangling keys
going past our cell door. My heart was pounding but
the only reassurance I could give myself was that the
cell door was firmly locked and no-one was getting in.
(The Secret Prisoner)[2]

The deprivation of physical and psychological security
can be immediate. Newly arrived prisoners have to
adapt quickly to a physical and social environment
which threatens harm and generates anxiety, even if they
have been in prison before. There is a myriad of rules to
learn, and failure to understand prison routines might
mean losing the chance to get some fresh air or missing
a phone call to a loved one. Prisoners are surrounded by
unknown people of whom they have good reason to be
wary. People who end up incarcerated are more likely
to display impulsivity and anger, perhaps exacerbated
by mental health problems or substance misuse. Staff
have substantial power and carry weapons such as
batons and pepper spray, and it can be a frightening
experience to witness forcible restraint.

Many prisoners will be worrying about the outcome
of their case or despondent about their sentence,
and they may be upset about separation from their
children or partner. Their feelings may be heightened
by noise, sleep deprivation, pre-existing ill health,
and forced withdrawal from drugs, alcohol or
prescribed medication.

> The first thing that hits me is the noise: yelling, banging, screaming, grunting, begging, barking, threatening, ranting, laughing, trading, scoring, whining, arguing, fighting, howling, crying. It's as if someone has downloaded every single prison sound effect from the internet and is blaring them all out, dialled up to 11.[3]

This description is by no means an exaggeration. I once had an office on a landing in a busy local prison, and after everyone was locked up after their 'evening' meal – ridiculously, this is still commonly served around 4.30–5 pm in England and Wales – the banging on doors and shouting would start, carrying on until late at night and sometimes through the night. I have also frequently stood on a landing during the day barely able to hear someone in front of me speaking because of the sounds echoing through the wing. The heavy-duty materials used to construct prisons are designed to withstand violence and fire, rather than to create a normalized living environment or encourage conversation. Consider for a moment how much worse this could be for those who are neurodiverse and have an even stronger reaction to sensory stimuli (see Chapter 5).

In early 2023, I visited a unit called 'Little Scandinavia', part of the Chester State Correctional Institution near Philadelphia[4] and found a rare example of a meaningful effort to reduce the barrage of prison noise. The unit has been redesigned to encourage human interaction in line with the Scandinavian principles of 'normalization' (see Chapter 7) and staff had installed noise-absorbing ceiling discs, which greatly reduced the clang of the wing. It was amazing how this simple change, along with a few other modifications, had changed the atmosphere of the unit. Prisoners could sit and talk together easily in the communal areas of the unit, which included comfortable chairs and a kitchen where they could cook and eat together.

But more often the first experience of a Western prison will be closer to that described in the two previous quotes, despite efforts to give enhanced support to new arrivals through, for example, peer supporters and welfare interviews with staff. Conditions generally improve as people go through the system and enter more settled long-term or open prisons. The latter usually have more staff and more opportunities for work and education, although even the most effectively led and best-resourced prisons struggle to offer enough activity or social interaction to fill a purposeful day.

Mike's story

Mike was a successful white businessman in his late twenties with no previous convictions. I met him during one of my earliest prison roles, risk-assessing people who had just been remanded on murder or manslaughter charges. I wasn't assessing their risk of harm to others, but to themselves. Some of the biggest risk factors for suicide are conviction for a violent offence – especially homicide, facing a life sentence and entering custody, with the early days being especially risky.[5] Each of these criteria applied to Mike, who had killed a man after getting into a fight during a night out. I was particularly worried because the prison had been through several tragic 'runs' of suicides – nine people had died this way in one recent 12-month period.

When I first spoke to Mike, he was still in shock. He had been remanded into custody the previous day and found it hard to speak. He was distant and seemed to be struggling to know what to say or how to act in this new reality. As the weeks went by, self-recrimination, horror and fear about the future gradually set in. He was also finding it hard to adjust to the prison environment with its constant clamour, long periods locked up and lack of activity. Counselling services were scarce and he had very little contact with his family; I hoped the space I could give him to talk might help him to come to terms with his situation.

Mike admitted his offence, felt he should be punished and probably got a long sentence – I don't know how long because, as often happens in an overcrowded system, he was moved from my prison after one of his court hearings and that was the last I heard of him. The very particular circumstances of his case suggested he was unlikely to pose much of a danger to the general public, and retribution was the main reason for imprisoning him. The disabling effects of institutionalization and common degradations of communal prison life were likely to diminish his ability to reintegrate into the community successfully on release, potentially increasing the likelihood of reoffending. Imagining a different sentence to imprisonment is difficult in this case, and there may have been an outpouring of media and political rage if the judge had exacted retribution through community reparation instead of prison (see the Scottish case in Chapter 7).

Despair and suicide

An unmistakeable gloom descends on prisons when someone has just taken their own life. You can sense the pain of many prisoners and staff who are searching their memories to see if they could have done more to notice or prevent the person's death. The emotional impact on cellmates and friends, and on prison officers who find and cut down the dead person (hanging is a very common method of prison suicide), can be lifelong. In England and Wales, the office of the Prison and Probation Ombudsman (PPO) investigates all such deaths, providing detailed and often harrowing insights into individual stories. Consider the following:

> A distressed 18-year-old Lithuanian man who had been arrested for stealing sweets killed himself in the segregation unit. ... Mr Pagirys rang a bell in his cell in the segregation unit at lunchtime but it was not answered for 37 minutes, at which time he was found hanging, unconscious. He never regained consciousness and died three days later.[6]

The author Chris Atkins happened to be incarcerated in the same prison as this young man, and adds more personal dimension to this tragic event. Atkins was about to become a 'Listener', that is, a prisoner who is trained by the Samaritans to support people who are at risk of self-harm or suicide:

> Scott comes in looking extremely glum. 'There's been another suicide on the mains.' Details are thin, but apparently it was a Lithuanian teenager who had severe mental health problems. He was on remand for shoplifting sweets, and had been sent to the segregation block. ... Leroy is a ripped south London hood who ... was called to see Osvaldas Pagirys on the night before the Lithuanian killed himself ... Leroy is racked with guilt that he couldn't do more to save him. It's only now that I grasp the real risks of becoming a Listener. Wandsworth is full of desperately lost souls, and sharing their pain is likely to have a profoundly harrowing effect.[7]

A similar role to the Listener exists in US prisons, and the following account shows the power of human compassion and the support that prisoners give each other:

> The 18-year-old black kid I'm assigned to on this day is soft-spoken, and severely depressed. (I'm 43 and white.) He opens up surprisingly quickly about the many horrors of his childhood. He's lived a very hard life, which is typical for incarcerated people but is always deeply upsetting nonetheless. I almost cry several times. There's not much I can do for him except listen, so I do so as if this young man is my own child.[8]

Figure 6.1: A Listener in a UK prison

PPO investigations sometimes find that staff have done all that can reasonably be expected to prevent self-inflicted deaths, but it is more common for them to find a range of failures by individuals. The context and underlying dynamics of individual mistakes are given much less attention in most reports. But surely it is no coincidence that the most overcrowded, understaffed and run-down institutions are frequently cited as failing to protect prisoners at risk. These prisons are the most noisy and stressful, where it is difficult for prisoners to request or receive practical and emotional help from staff, or even get time with the Listeners, who do such an exceptional and difficult job.

The PPO report into the death of Osvaldas Pagirys catalogued a range of problems common to overstretched prisons, including poor healthcare assessment, lack of communication about risk between staff, lack of attention to individual needs and a slow response to emergency bells. This young man was vulnerable, far from home and could speak little English. Staff made very little use of professional interpretation and if they had, they might have understood how desperate he was and the fact that his mental health was deteriorating. The PPO concluded that his 'unpredictable, emotional and distressed behaviour' resulted in a punitive system response rather than a proper attempt to understand his distress – this is not unusual in prisons where people with mental health problems often have challenging behaviours which distract staff from their underlying vulnerability. But what was a disturbed 18-year-old who had taken sweets doing in one of the most forbidding prisons in the UK in the first place?

Dignity

Prisoners quickly learn to tolerate the regular, often small-scale assaults on dignity that are an everyday part of life in even the best prisons. Albert Woodfox, who was in solitary confinement for over forty years for an offence he did not commit, vividly describes the loss of agency and individuality:

> In prison, you are part of a human herd. In the human herd survival of the fittest is all there is. You become instinctive, not intellectual. Therein lies the secret to the master's control. One minute you're treated like a baby,

being handed a spoon to eat with or being told where to stand. The next, with utter indifference, you're being counted several times a day—you have no choice, you have no privacy. The next moment you're threatened, pushed, tested.[9]

A very basic example of the struggle to achieve dignity in prison relates to fundamental need to go to the toilet. This is often in a shared cell with a lightly screened or completely open toilet:

I went for my first official pee in jail. This felt awkward in itself, like Bobby [cellmate] was watching and listening to every last little drip. Stage fright took over and it felt like an eternity to finish the stream ... the biggest bonus of being alone was finally being able to go to the toilet by myself, relax and relieve myself from the stomach pains, embarrassment of poo'ing in front of someone and gain a little bit of dignity back.[10]

The strip search is a prison practice that takes place the world over. This may entail the prisoner taking off the bottom half and top half of their clothes separately, but in many countries they are totally naked. Prisoners often have to squat in case anything is concealed between the buttocks, in the anus or vagina. Strip searches can result in weapons, drugs and phones being discovered, which to varying degrees can make a prison extremely dangerous. I know that many prison staff try hard to be as sensitive as possible, but strip-searching is intrinsically intrusive and stressful, especially for women who are particularly likely to have been victims of sexual violence (see Chapter 5).

As we have already seen, gender is integral to the experience of prison and to the power that prison staff can wield over people's bodies and minds. In a Kenyan prison I visited, women were subject to humiliating public strip searches and required to squat for visual inspection by staff in front of all the others in their dormitory. Oddly, strip-searching was done in private in the men's prisons and another women's prison I saw, but local practices had endured. By far the worst case of abusive prison strip-searching that I have come across was on the Dutch Caribbean island of Aruba.[11] A suspicion of illicit items entering the prison had led to the director ordering a search of the entire female prisoner population – not just a strip search, but also a 'cavity' search, that is, medical personnel physically examining a woman's vagina and anus. In some cases, the women understandably refused to cooperate, including at least one who had previously experienced sexual violence, but they were searched by force in a room with male officers present. Cavity searching was at one point a routine practice in the US system:

> The 'internal search' was as humiliating and disgusting as it sounded. You sit on the edge of this table and the nurse holds your legs open and sticks a finger in your vagina and moves it around. She has a plastic glove on. Some of them try to put one finger in your vagina and another one up your rectum at the same time.[12]

In his analysis of the degradations of the prison strip-search, Albert Woodfox once again illustrates the powerful echoes of slavery in the US system:

> I'd learned enough about chattel slavery to see a connection between the unnecessary strip searches for CCR prisoners and how African American men and women were treated as slaves. Forced to strip down on the auction block before they were bought and sold, black men and women had their bodies, mouths, and genitals inspected for disease as if they were livestock. It's one of the most humiliating experiences a human being can endure ... The strip search always entailed a visual cavity search. After removing our clothes, we had to open our mouths, raise our scrotum, lift our feet to show the bottoms, turn around, bend over, and spread our buttocks ...
> The chances of a fully clothed man being able to hide contraband in his anus while handcuffed in the front to his waist were zero. Under these circumstances strip searches were merely another unnecessary cruelty.[13]

These cases show the potential for abuses that would be considered outrageous outside the prison to be perpetrated with impunity inside the prison walls. Do we really need to continue strip-searching in the twenty-first century? Most staff I speak to hate strip-searching as much as the prisoners and, in England and Wales, technology is starting to bring into question the need for such a procedure. Many prisons are now installing airport-style scanners that can pick up contraband without the need to remove clothing, and have a 'body orifice security scanner' (known as the 'BOSS' chair), which can detect mobile phones or electrical equipment hidden in the body. If these methods were available to all, it should greatly reduce reliance on a practice whose negative effects arguably outweigh any security gains.

Identity

> All prisoners have their identity stripped from them and, ultimately, reconstructed by the institutions in which they are incarcerated. (Jason Warr)[14]

More than most social environments, prison encourages people to project a manufactured sense of themselves, often with a strong dose of bravado or, by contrast, a constriction of personality as they retreat into themselves because of fear or depression. Longer sentences are routinely imposed in the US and increasingly common in the UK,[15] bringing further challenges as the person strives to show the authorities that they are worthy of release. This may encourage a genuine development of personality – like any environment, the prison changes you and can do so positively. Or it can lead to a performance, played out, for example, through technical participation in programmes designed to change attitudes and behaviour, without any intention to learn from them. Criminologist Ben Crewe uses the evocative concept of the 'penal avatar', which prisoners feel they must create to progress through the system:

> Often, they feel that cognitive-behavioural courses are telling them to be a different kind of person – at worst, a robotic prototype of responsible citizenship that could not survive the realities of life in the environments from which they are drawn.[16]

Jason Warr, himself a former long-term prisoner, found that young, indeterminately sentenced prisoners (those with no fixed release date) adopted 'an institutionally acceptable form of their self' in an attempt to show they were being rehabilitated.[17] While there can be little argument with giving people in prison the chance to think about and discuss the behaviours that led to them being imprisoned, these researchers warn of the dangers of rehabilitation becoming a game in which prisoners simply act out parts.

Similarly, in a study I led in England and Wales, Black prisoners, who are much more likely than other groups to have force used against them, said they felt vulnerable around white staff and dealt with problems of trust and communication through three main strategies: *avoidance* of staff, *resignation* to the way they were treated, or *adaptation*. The latter generally meant changing the way they normally communicated, adjusting their speech and behaviour because they believed that would result in fairer treatment. One prisoner described this as 'sounding white' to be more accepted.[18]

The pains of imprisonment

Modern prisons may deliver pain differently and with more subtlety than in the past, but they do it with impressive consistency – it is their undisputed strength. The rehabilitative role of prisons is by contrast largely dispensable, as demonstrated by the wholesale removal in many of the world's prisons of work, education, exercise, family visits and rehabilitative programmes during the COVID-19 pandemic; and their regular withdrawal whenever there is a shortage of staff, funds or political will.

Much of the thinking and research about the pains of imprisonment in the West was sparked by the classic 1958 account of the US sociologist and criminologist Gresham Sykes, *The Society of Captives*.[19] Sykes identified five broad 'deprivations' of prison life: liberty, goods and services, heterosexual relationships, autonomy and security, all of which I have referenced in different parts of this book. This groundbreaking but dated work – for example it makes assumptions about heterosexual orientation and says very little about women – has been updated by others, with much more attention now paid to the psychological pains of imprisonment and the diversity of prisoners.

Especially notable is criminologist Ben Crewe's research, in which he develops the concepts of the 'depth, weight and tightness'. He suggests that during Sykes' time prisons were generally focused on security, control and prevention of escapes, with strict rules and routines, making them 'deep' and 'heavy'. But they were also 'loose', because few demands were made on prisoners to do anything other than serve their time. He argues that in the 1970s and 1980s, UK prisons became 'heavier', with a more malign culture to add to the indifference, and very poor material prison conditions. All of this helps to explain the waves of disturbances that followed the UK's biggest riot at Strangeways prison in 1990, which lasted about three weeks and caused much official soul-searching.[20] Crewe uses the term 'tightness' to describe how people are suppressed or 'wrapped up' to get them to act in particular ways, and refers to research by McDermott and King, in which prisoners told them, 'They don't beat us any more – they don't have to. They can win by using paper. It's all a mind game now.'[21] This 'softening of penal power' is, Crewe argues, more salient today, given that far more prisoners are serving long sentences which produce 'feelings of uncertainty, dependence and disorientation', while paperwork about matters such as recategorization, transfer or early release increasingly shapes the prison experience.[22]

Another way to put this is that the requirements of prison bureaucracy can be a sanitized form of delivering the pains of imprisonment. I have often heard staff who don't have time to talk to prisoners – or don't want to talk to them – telling them to 'fill in an application' (for example, to see a probation officer or to obtain their property); or to 'make a formal complaint', ostensibly to encourage them to use systems that are supposed to support and safeguard prisoners. But responses and appeals can take several weeks, and the forms can be hard to understand, especially for the many prisoners with poor literacy and numeracy, denting their morale and motivation. Many prisons in England and Wales are attempting to deal with this by emphasizing informal resolution of problems, that is staff and prisoners simply talking to each other, but success is uneven and undermined by a lack of staff. There is also the serious, Kafkaesque problem of people being given sentence targets which they are told they must achieve to be considered for early release, but then having no chance of success because the required courses are not available.[23]

People who need prison?

'I felt a great sense of relief when I was sentenced. Life outside had been such a disaster, painful for me and more importantly for others because of me. I was glad it was over ... I reflected for the first time over long hours on what I had become and tried to make sense of how I could have behaved the way I did.'[24] (Erwin James)

Erwin James had no affinity for prison but at the start of his sentence he felt he needed to be behind bars. Many prisoners describe the value of getting away from destructive patterns of behaviour, which might include drug or alcohol misuse, unhealthy relationships and violence. Despite the stress and dangers of imprisonment, it can be worse for them outside and a relief to have decision-making and responsibilities removed. Prison can also help people to mature and gain control of poor mental health that leads to offending. The following comment, made in 2022, is from a man with a diagnosed mental illness who was 17 years into a sentence for serious violent offences:

> I can honestly say up until 2020, I was not ready to be released. If you put me back into the community again, I'd have reoffended in a heartbeat. I didn't know anything, I didn't know who I was, I didn't understand my illness. So coming to prison, I know it sounds cliched, it was one the best things that ever happened to me. I've got a routine, I've got structure.[25]

This does not mean that prison is not painful or that it is the only way to respond to serious offending, but it provides a more complete depiction that can help us to understand its enduring appeal.

Some people appear to function better in prison. Carl was a bright, cheerful and popular white man in his early thirties. He found it easy to talk to people and spent a lot of time mediating between prisoners who needed help and staff who might be able to provide it. He was employed as an orderly (a trusted role similar to that of a Listener) supporting other prisoners with a range of practical problems, and he did the job very well. Carl had a string of convictions for burglaries committed to fund long-term drug use that started during an unsettled childhood. He had sought help from the prison drug support service and did not appear to be taking drugs when I knew him.

I sometimes saw Carl upset at the aggression, petty behaviours and frustrating bureaucracy he encountered in prison, but it also gave him a sense of community and purpose that he struggled to achieve elsewhere. Prison was clearly not a long-term solution to his behaviours and had not 'worked' well enough to help him keep out of trouble. He had not been released for long when I saw him again, once again in good spirits and busy helping people, but back in the same prison for very similar offending after a relapse into drug misuse.

In prison, Carl followed the rehabilitation script. He took the opportunity to help people in need, while gaining meaning and motivation during what could otherwise seem a wasted prison existence. An unanswered question was, why could he not find these things on release?

Erwin James felt he was close to giving up on himself in prison because he was there for so long, but was released before he reached the point of no return. He gives an eloquent and balanced view of how those working in prison helped him to develop:

> I adapted well to life inside. It was often bleak and unbearably stressful; the mental pressures were immense. But there were, and are, some great people who work in those places who want to help people like me to function properly, not just for the sake of those who cause harm and distress to others, but for the sake of all of us. I gravitated towards those life-enhancing people and will be forever grateful to them. I began to see prison as a potentially beneficial community and in wider terms, a valuable community resource. ... Don't get me wrong: besides the

> positive opportunities, there were mind games, politics,
> riots, sieges, suicides, stabbings and killings – anybody
> who argues that prison life, especially long-term prison life,
> is a 'holiday camp' has no understanding of the issue.[26]

So, notwithstanding the pains of life inside, prison can do some good. The question is, could the behaviours have been prevented or the self-destructive cycles interrupted without the prison? Something I hear over and again from prisoners is that they needed, but didn't receive, early intervention from people with the time and skills to guide them away from the negative trajectories they were on. The intervention might involve easily available community centres for young people where they can get the mentoring and sense of belonging that might help them avoid the destructive path to imprisonment. Or it might entail much more intensive support once someone enters prison for the first time to prevent a recurrence:

> I so wished I'd had more help and support when I was
> a teenager in the detention centre, or later in the borstal
> system. I'd needed help so badly.[27]

But what happens when we are presented with someone who did not get such support when it might have made a difference, and is not willing or able to listen or desist? What if, like Erwin James and many others, they need a 'hard break' – that is, a forceful intervention to take them away from their lifestyle because they are too incapable, unhappy, angry, unconcerned or arrogant to care about making changes? What would that look like, if not prison?

The stories in this chapter and Chapter 5 reflect the diverse and intense experiences that make up the emotional world of prisons. For some, prison is welcome and even transformative, at least for a time, while for others it is degrading and brutalizing. It may have all of these effects on the same person at different times. In the next chapter, we will explore different ideas about the future of the prison, and what alternative visions of behaviour management might look like.

7

WHERE NEXT FOR PRISONS?

The prison of my childhood imagination that I spoke about in the opening chapter has long since disappeared. Prisons are no longer places of fear or strangeness for me, and prisoners have become the real people they always were. But experience and knowledge can also drive out clarity, and this final chapter is my attempt to reach towards a more complete understanding of the prison conundrum. We will touch on the loose positions I set out in the first chapter (penal enthusiasm, abolitionism and liberal reform), but rather than building a case for any of them, I will try to provide information and raise questions. First, we will briefly rehearse what we know so far about the purposes of prison:

- All prisons deliver retributive pain through deprivation of liberty and separation from family and community.
- Harm defines the prison experience even more completely. People are usually in prison because they have harmed others, and any benefits of prison generally come with a generous dose of harm to prisoners and their communities.
- Prisons perform an important protective function by incapacitating some very dangerous people who are likely to inflict extreme harm on others if they are not forcibly prevented.
- For people who need an escape route from lives that are spiralling out of control, prisons may provide a useful combination of control and support and can be beneficial to the offender and to society in the short term.
- But imprisonment has a weak overall effect on reducing crime. Even if you imprison very large numbers of people, there is a short-term depressant effect on crime, but it is not substantial, comes at great social and economic cost, and probably doesn't last for long. A more sophisticated analysis of crime production that can measure the intergenerational effects of imprisonment may show no link at all.
- Prison is overwhelmingly used to hold the socially marginalized and the economically disadvantaged, and these structural afflictions are usually reinforced and perpetuated by incarceration.

- Prison does not deter much crime, but a reasonable likelihood of being caught does.
- Prison has a poor record of rehabilitating people. There is a persistently flimsy commitment to this purpose of prison and even for the healthy and resilient, the prison experience undermines successful integration into society. It removes individual agency, and most prisons do little to encourage people towards new thinking and creativity in addressing old problems in their lives.
- We cannot understand the purpose of prison by looking at it in isolation from the objectives of those in charge of the state. It is one of the most formidable means of political control that states possess, as illustrated, for example, by the history of racialized incarceration in the US.

So, prison incapacitates some people who pose a very high risk of harm to others. It rehabilitates a small number of people. It deters a small number. It punishes and exacts retribution rather effectively for a larger number. While achieving these modest outcomes, it tends to reproduce and embed disadvantage and weakens communities, thereby at least partially undermining any gains.

Some readers – those I simplistically labelled in the opening chapter as penal enthusiasts – will see the latter as collateral damage to the purposes of retributive punishment. They may also see wide-scale imprisonment as inevitable because there is no obvious alternative. Others, the liberal reformers, will be more concerned about the failure of virtually every prison system around the world to provide consistently decent and humane conditions, and their equally poor record of delivering effective rehabilitation. Going a step further than reformers, the abolitionists see prison as intrinsically problematic institutions which buttress inequality and obstruct deeper social change.

I will now briefly explore each of these positions with a view to offering a selective critical commentary. Regardless of our starting point in the debate, the aim is to help consideration of new perspectives.

The roots of penal enthusiasm: is prison inevitable?

Despite its contradictions, abuses and operational problems, no government, no matter how radical, has dispensed with the prison, and no popular movement has ever persuaded a government to commit to prison abolition. On the contrary, it is more likely that popular demands for protection from crime and social disorder will motivate governments to use the prison even more extensively. The prison's umbilical connection to the idea of moral order is illustrated daily by cultural products, such as films and computer games, which endlessly rehearse the ultimate victory of the good guys over the baddies who end up dead or behind bars. The 'ideology' of the prison[1] shows little sign of loosening its grip, supporting Foucault's belief that as prison is a concentrated reflection of other institutions in society which exercise discipline and control (schools, reformatories, the army and even employment), it seemed almost instantly obvious and inevitable when first invented. But how inevitable is it really?

A common argument of penal enthusiasts is that liberal reformers and abolitionists fail the most vulnerable and the poorest by refusing to support the victims who want offenders off the streets. Those victims tend to come from the same deprived areas as offenders and want a quick outcome, namely to send away the person who has caused them harm. To take an extreme but illustrative example, in El Salvador rival gangs had terrorized whole communities until there was a brutal, and in some respects illegal, crackdown on gang members. The action taken by the government was hugely popular and brought peace and stability to many people. The human rights abuses entailed by this use of the prison were not in dispute but, to put it bluntly, few people cared, given the benefits.[2]

A deeper analysis suggests that the reaction to these events should perhaps not be to celebrate the effectiveness of prison or the decisiveness of the government, but to understand that prison was a desperate last resort to address a crisis that should never have happened in the first place. We would then need to ask why society had become so dysfunctional and social bonds so weak, that membership of violent gangs became highly attractive to young people (see Chapter 4 on the growth of Brazilian prison gangs). This would allow us to understand the circumstances that lead to crime, and prevent them in the future. The problem is, of course, that most people understandably want quick solutions to immediate problems of community safety. Social change takes a long time and is an investment in the future rather than a solution for the present. We therefore tend to see a less extreme version of the El Salvador dynamic around the world, where governments use prisons to mop up, often tardily and always temporarily, problems that originate in the nature of society and may have been created by the policies of those very same governments. A sensible debate about fundamental questions of purpose is not a high priority in this context.

Another argument for the prison is that it is now so closely associated with just punishment that without it, people would lose faith in the ability of the state to protect us, creating a disordered and brutal society. The legal philosopher Joel Feinberg talks about punishment in general as 'a symbolic way of getting back at the criminal, of expressing a kind of vindictive resentment'.[3] Punishment therefore has an important *expressive* function, and as prison is the apex of punitive response to crime in most states, it has an almost irresistible attraction to individuals and societies seeking an antidote to the insecurities of the modern world. In other words, regardless of the unequal way in which it operates, prison has become so popular for reasons that go far beyond racism and class oppression, although those nefarious motivations are also present. It marks the state's disapproval of people who break its norms, and appeals to the disadvantaged as well as the powerful. So, can anything else dislodge its hegemony?

The discussion in Chapters 5 and 6 may help us to move towards a greater sense of the individual in the criminal justice process and an understanding that offenders can experience the same objective punishment very differently. This idea opens the way to a more complex view of retribution – one that does not equate the term 'punishment' with 'prison', and ceases to reinforce the erroneous idea that only deprivation of liberty can deliver retributive pain.[4] There is, for example, good evidence that community sentences are experienced as being punitive while also being more effective at reducing crime, especially when they replace short sentences and when they are used for young offenders.[5] I have lost count of the number of people, usually persistent offenders, who have told me they would rather have a prison sentence than a community order, so they can just get the punishment 'out of the way', rather than have to endure the lengthier, and to them more burdensome, period of surveillance, challenge and self-reflection usually required by probation oversight.

But, in general, if retributive punishment is what is required of a sentence, prison clearly outmuscles any other response short of the death penalty, and no end of punitive reforms to community sentences will change that. It is only when we move out of this restricted conceptual space that there is scope for a genuinely different approach in which punishment is not seen as the main goal of sentencing and is replaced, for example, by reducing reoffending or reparation.

Elements of this debate have been played out in the Scottish Government's recent attempt to undermine the hegemony of the prison with new sentencing guidelines for young people that focus squarely on the goal of rehabilitation rather than retribution, and will generally mean not sending them to prison at all. The guidance draws on research showing that young people are likely to have a lower level of maturity and 'a greater capacity for change and rehabilitation'.[6] The difficulty of enacting policies aimed at something other than punishment is illustrated by the dismay and anger from campaigning and victim support groups, lawyers, politicians and press that accompanied the community sentence given to a 17-year-old who raped a 13-year-old girl.[7] The judge stated that this serious crime would have a long-lasting impact on the victim, but that imprisonment was unlikely to support the rehabilitation of the offender (now aged 21), who had a history of mental health problems and substance abuse. The judge followed the guidelines and focused on reducing future risk of harm but in so doing he was attacked for failing to show enough punitive retribution on behalf of society. If this attempt at changing the penal landscape continues, it will be a difficult transition for all concerned, including groups usually considered to be natural supporters of decarceration.

Exploring abolition

Abolition is not primarily concerned with the prison itself. It is about changing society so that the prison becomes, in Angela Davis's words, 'obsolete'[8]. A purist version of abolitionism eschews attempts at reforming the prison because that merely legitimates an incoherent and ineffective institution. As discussed later in this section, this position is modified by abolitionists who are often in favour of prison reforms as long as they are 'non-reformist', that is, they do not entrench the power of the prison.

Abolitionism comes into very sharp focus in the US, where its momentum is due partly to the mass incarceration discussed in Chapter 4, which traces precise lines between prison and slavery, racism, social inequality and mistreatment of marginalized groups. Explicitly state-sanctioned racism in the US is so recent (racial segregation was only outlawed in 1964), and the debate about racism and incarceration has been articulated in such a vibrant intellectual and popular culture by thinkers like Davis, that it becomes difficult to see prison as anything other than a means of enforcing iniquitous hierarchies.

But there is no evidence that the abolitionist vision of an egalitarian society would necessarily lead to the obsolescence of the prison. While circumstances such as poverty and racism influence who commits, and is arrested for, crime, it is pure speculation that a just society would necessarily lead to an absence of the most harmful crimes. Perhaps reflecting such gaps in theory, there is considerably more nuance in abolitionist circles than is often assumed. Some abolitionists now believe that, at least in the short to medium term, prison is socially necessary to address very serious crime and ongoing dangerous behaviour.

Abolitionists have a more immediate focus on creating a more socially just and egalitarian society which, they assume, will eventually remove the conditions that lead to the use of prison. Such a society would no longer create and reinforce disadvantage, and prison would no longer be used as a means of protecting the powerful. A more socially advanced society should also be capable of developing better ways of managing violence outside of the prison through, for example, advanced forms of community reparation based on principles of mutual care.

Rather than 'What are prisons for?', abolitionists tend to ask a more fundamental and in some ways far simpler question: 'How can we prevent and constructively address the harm caused by people who break laws, without either causing further harm to them, their families and communities; or allowing the state and society to avoid its share of responsibility for individual behaviours and ignoring its ability to promote change?'

This may be hard to comprehend, but visions of new social realities are, by definition, difficult to imagine while we are living in a profoundly different present. Reforming prisons is a much easier idea because it does not challenge our foundational thinking in the same way.

The immediate objective of abolitionists is to remove the harm caused by the prison, and the question of what might replace any of its useful functions is a lesser priority, although not one that has been ignored. For example, in the context of the UK's ageing prison population and concerns about the welfare of older people in prison, a non-reformist approach suggested by abolitionist Sarah Lamble is to push for early or compassionate release rather than calling for specialized prison geriatric services.[9] Pat Carlen echoes the non-reformist position in her discussion of women's prison reform. She suggests a range of alternatives, including women's courts which provide treatment, support, development of living skills and regular reports to the court, and individualized programmes designed for women.[10] Carlen articulates an important element of the non-prison-legitimating approach to reform as follows:

> If the sentencing pull of prison is to be effectively
> confronted ... it is essential that imprisonment be uncoupled
> from any kind of 'treatment', 'restorative' or 'rehabilitative'
> thinking; and that in future it is unambiguously recognised
> for what it is: a place where punishment by confinement
> is forever aggravated by the inevitable pains of regimes
> primarily, and necessarily, organised to keep prisoners in.[11]

The problem with this argument is that it takes rather a narrow view of rehabilitation. A decent, humane prison where people have good relationships fits with the broader idea of what has become known in England and Wales as 'rehabilitative culture'.[12] The emphasis of this approach is not on any specific intervention designed to promote rehabilitation, or on advertising the prison as a desirable place of individual reform. But once there, the focus is on change through a safe and supportive environment and building the human relationships that research suggests can motivate people towards change. Admittedly, outside of Norway, I would not confidently describe any prison that I have seen as 'rehabilitative', but, with a few disturbing exceptions, nor have I seen prisons that are entirely places of pain and containment. A prison that fits that description was in Tripoli, Lebanon (before it reached its current dire economic situation), where 70 people were crammed into cells barely big enough for 20.[13] They had little natural light, only one toilet, and were let out of the cell once every few days. The air was acrid with cigarette smoke and bodily odours. There were so few guards that trusted prisoners held keys for everything except the outer gates, including the 1 m × 1.5 m isolation and punishment cell where anyone who displeased them could end up. I fear this is the logical end point of a prison that aspires, as Carlen suggests, to do nothing but contain.

In Norway, prison officials described the function of the prison to me as rehabilitation and reducing reoffending, but looked a little blank when I asked them about offending behaviour programmes to help them achieve this outcome. My question was obviously too narrowly conceived. While programmes were offered, the main rehabilitative intervention was staff talking to prisoners about their lives and goals. Alongside deep professional relationships, the emphasis was on providing education, therapy, and a decent and safe environment. Prisoners did not like being in prison, but every one I spoke to felt they were benefiting from the approach taken; the low Norwegian reoffending rate shows that the community was also benefiting.

So, I think prison will inevitably incorporate the notion of rehabilitation, and ultimately that means the seeds for prison growth remain intact, as they have done for the hundreds of years. We either need to acccpt that or do something entirely different.

More liberal reform?

A common goal for those who want reform without abolition is to reduce the numbers going to prison, as in Finland, and focus instead on improving conditions and providing better treatment and support services in prisons. This is more or less what liberal reformers in the West have been trying to do for the last 300 years. A risk of this strategy is what has become known as 'carceral humanism'.[14] The term describes how mental health and other services are increasingly targeted 'behind the walls', thereby diverting money from already underfunded provision in communities. The concern is that this sustains the supply line to prisons while giving the false impression that at some point enough therapeutic resource will be made available to make prison a suitable place of treatment and rehabilitation. Such thinking may influence the sentencing of people like Karen (see Chapter 5), who was rarely safe in the community and needed a way out. The great shame of it is that prison, with its inherent risks and degradations, was seen as the most viable option to achieve that goal.

Norway is often cited as an exemplar of a liberal reform and appears to be a good counter to the carceral humanism argument as it has both improved services in prison and kept its prison population relatively low. Norway has made substantial progress in reducing reoffending through an approach that explicitly rejects the idea of prison as exclusion. The goal from the day of first entry is instead to return people to the community in a better position to avoid reoffending. It currently has a reconviction rate of 20 per cent after two years, which is a vast drop from the 60–70 per cent that it reported in the 1990s,[15] garnering international approval even from some traditional critics of its liberal prison regimes.[16]

Norway has a tradition of small prisons which are integrated into communities. I visited one holding 16 people that took up the ground floor of a private apartment block, and another that held 13, which was located opposite a block of luxury apartments. Both were in residential areas close to shops and playgrounds, and the prisoners, nearly all of whom had committed serious violent and sexual offences, were able to go out with or sometimes without staff on day release. This is in line with the Norwegian principle of 'normalization', which is creating conditions as similar as possible to what would be experienced in the community because the smaller the difference between life inside and outside, the more likelihood there is of a safe transition.

It is understood that people will eventually leave prison, and one popular catchphrase repeated by prison staff and campaigners is: 'Who do you want for your neighbour?' The expected answer is someone who has undergone work to support rehabilitation and reintegration before their release. Prison officers are highly trained over a period of two years and focus on building relationships with prisoners that can help them to progress.

Overcrowding prisons is a worldwide malaise which creates inhumane conditions and takes away all pretence of the prison being for any purpose other than containment. Prisoners suffer from it and everyone I know who works in prison is sick of it. Offenders in Norway must wait until prisons have enough space to accommodate them before they start their sentence. As well as keeping prison numbers down and reducing costs, I was told by Norwegian prison reformers that this was also a useful encouragement for judges to consider other sentences that could be imposed more swiftly.

Of course, even the Norwegian model is no panacea and recent research has reasserted the pains of Norwegian incarceration.[17] Abolitionists might also point out that its achievements have been in an already comparatively egalitarian, high trust, low fear and wealthy society, all of which tend to reduce crime and imprisonment. In most other parts of the world, recidivism rates are so high (59 per cent in England and Wales for example[18]) that prisons could be considered criminogenic.

There are ways to narrow the gap between reformers and abolitionists. One example might be ending prison sentences for non-violent offences and finding other ways to manage persistent thieves, burglars and drug offenders like Karen (Chapter 5) and Carl (Chapter 6), including through community control measures and treatment services. This approach would also prevent imprisonment for the purposes of border control (see Jayden's story in Chapter 3). The Nordic countries once again provide some examples of how this might be achieved through their extensive use of conditional and suspended sentences, community supervision, community service and treatment orders and, increasingly, electronic monitoring (EM).[19] There are still few studies of EM and they vary in rigour, but they support cautious optimism about its value in reducing reoffending when used as a direct alternative to prison.[20] In Norway, EM is accompanied by a requirement for structured demands such as education and employment programmes, unpaid and paid work, or drug treatment, which can add up to the equivalent of a full working week. In their Norwegian study, Andersen and Telle found that replacing prison with EM led to a 15 per cent reduction in reoffending after one and two years.[21]

A more radical option might be the use of prison for safety and public protection only, that is for people who are assessed as posing an immediate risk of serious harm to others in the community, and not necessarily those who have *already* committed violent offences. The retributive element of imprisonment would be fulfilled through community restrictions and reparation. This would mean people like Mike (Chapter 6) would not go to prison. Community penalties would be the first option for even the most serious offences and much more weight would be given to the opinions of risk assessment professionals such as probation officers, psychologists and psychiatrists, although some challenges of this approach are highlighted by the Scottish case discussed previously.

Too much democracy?

As the case of Finland has shown, expert-led policy appears to work. A logical conclusion might be that enlightened government officials and experts would do well to find ways, as Dzur, Loader and Sparks put it, of 'protecting punishment from democracy',[22] by restricting the public's say in complex matters of penal policy, so they can get on with implementing more rational policies of their choice. The notion that democracy in the US and elsewhere is too powerful and fickle an influence on penal policy is, to say the least, a problematic sub-narrative to prison critiques.

The fact that people in deprived communities – who are incidentally more likely to be victims of crime[23] – disproportionately fall within this inconvenient category, makes the idea of enlightened policy makers finding a route around them even less palatable. Furthermore, people who approve of punitive policies may well have knowledge of the research evidence but are more interested in knowing that those who have caused them or others loss, fear and distress, or may do so in the future, are locked up and excluded from the community even if it is for a short time. The 'expressive' nature of punishment (which makes them *feel* better) may be more important to them than evidence on long-term outcomes. These are perfectly legitimate and widespread perspectives.

Constructive ways should therefore be found to engage with the damage of mass incarceration without undermining democracy or implying, however unintentionally, that victims of crime should not be heard. Dzur, Loader and Sparks suggest a variety of responses that go well beyond providing more information for the general public, which may have little effect anyway for the reasons given previously. They suggest an extension of the critique of mass incarceration through a focus on democratic ideals; one obvious challenge could be to the removal of voting rights from citizens who have broken the law. Disenfranchising people in prison sends the message that they are no longer part of the national community, or at least not an important part of it; this imposed identity can persist on release, reducing their ability to reintegrate and lead a productive life. A critique of the impact of disenfranchising people should only be a starting point, they argue, for a broader investigation of how US penal policy is anti-democratic as it 'violates the democratic imperatives of voice, responsiveness, and accountability'.[24] Such theoretically coherent approaches will be vital to driving progress.

Concluding thoughts

A few weeks ago, I was sitting in a prison office, staring out of the window and thinking about how to deliver bad inspection findings to a capable and hard-working prison governor. The task is never easy and made harder when it's not obvious how prison leaders can significantly improve outcomes in overcrowded and underfunded institutions with too few and often inexperienced staff. I have a vague sense of inadequacy and responsibility, perhaps even complicity, in these situations. Writing this book has helped me to better understand those feelings.

Prisons are physically imposing structures, but their history, legacy and ideology loom even larger. Quite deliberately, they dominate both body and the mind, and offer an appealingly simple solution (exclusion) to any number of complex social problems. They pull us into their mythology so effectively that it feels almost impossible to imagine a different reality. Yet, the multitudinal purposes of prison make it almost impossible to answer what ought to be a fundamental question for any organization: 'What does "good" look like?'

Of course, some prisons are much better than others at delivering outcomes such as safety or meaningful activity that can help prepare people for release. But, for me, very few come close to meeting the test of a good prison I have often heard applied by prison staff: 'Would I be happy if my family member was held here?'[25] In fact, the more I try to imagine 'good', the less I am thinking about virtually every prison I have ever seen.

Perhaps we need to ask different and more fundamental questions to move towards a coherent set of ideas around purpose. The prisons itself should not be the starting point for this venture. Instead, we should begin at the beginning and ask:

- 'How can we reduce crime?'
- 'How can we reduce harm, including to people who break the law?'
- 'How can we prevent the criminal justice system from reinforcing social inequality, and instead make it a means of promoting equality?'
- 'How can we best achieve the socially useful functions of prisons?'
- 'Does punishment require the prison?'

I hope that whatever debate these questions inspire about the future of prisons does not take place entirely in echo chambers. In the interests of democratic progress, I would add a further question: 'How can we find accommodation with people who disagree with us?' For example, abolitionism provides a driving vision that can inspire criminal justice practitioners and reformers to think in original ways. And people who believe wholeheartedly in the prison as an effective way to protect society can ensure the experience of individual victims is never lost in prison reform debates that can sometimes become too theoretical.

In any event, if you have made it this far into the book, you are unlikely to believe, if you ever did, that the prison is designed simply to punish, deter and reform people who have broken society's rules, even though it may do these things too. It has many other functions that take place under the cover of legitimating terms such as public protection, rehabilitation or national security. It supports objectives as varied as nation-building, conquest and teaching literacy. It is a tremendously malleable manifestation of state power, preventing some harm but probably causing even more. The vast majority of prisons are good at keeping people in and mediocre or poor at everything else.

Policy makers and practitioners are usually concerned with short-term management of the system rather than long-term change based on the kind of historical insight and critical analysis that I have tried to provide in this book. But without an informed vision of possible futures, it is difficult to see how prison systems will emerge from seemingly perpetual crisis. That vision is primarily the responsibility of political leaders and others with political influence, and the experiences of countries such as Finland and Norway, and the UK in the first part of the twentieth century, may help to fire their imaginations. Maybe we need to have a second Enlightenment to get us thinking differently about prisons: this time, understanding why we have been so attached to them, cutting through, and preferably cutting out, the mythologies of prison that have held sway for so long.

I realized fairly quickly that I was never going to deliver a neatly packaged answer in this book to the question 'What are prisons for?'. But I now think that offering a way out of the mental shackles of prison ideology is what it can most usefully offer. Knowledge is indeed power, and understanding the prison is the first step towards improving it or improving on it.

NOTES

Chapter 1

1   Michael Howard, 'Prison works', Conservative Party conference speech, Blackpool, 6 October 1993.

2   Angela Y. Davis, *Are Prisons Obsolete?* (Seven Stories Press, 2003), p. 16.

3   HM Inspectorate of Prisons (HMIP), *Life in Prison: The First 24 Hours in Prison* (HMIP, 2015), p. 12, https://www. justiceinspectorates.gov.uk/hmiprisons/wp-content/uploads/ sites/4/2015/11/HMIP-First-24-hours-findings-paper-web-2015.pdf

4   Slogan coined by Tony Blair when Labour Shadow Home Secretary, and often repeated after the Labour Party came to power in the UK in 1997.

5   See Hindpal Bhui, *Going the Distance* (Prison Reform Trust, 2004), https://prisonreformtrust.org.uk/wp-content/uploads/2004/02/ GOING_THE_DISTANCE.pdf

6   See Alex South, *Behind These Doors* (Hodder and Stoughton, 2023) for an insightful and compassionate memoir of a prison officer's work.

7   See Hindpal Bhui, 'Anti-racist practice in NOMS: Reconciling managerialist and professional realities', *Howard Journal of Criminal Justice* 45 (2006), pp. 171–90.

8   Sir William Macpherson, *The Stephen Lawrence Inquiry* (The Stationery Office, 1999).

9   See Hindpal Bhui, 'Prisons and race equality', in Hindpal Bhui (ed) *Race and Criminal Justice* (Sage Publications, 2009), pp. 83–101.

10 Natasha A. Frost and Todd R. Clear, 'Theories of mass incarceration', in John D. Wooldredge and Paula Smith (eds), *The Oxford Handbook of Prisons and Imprisonment* (Oxford University Press, 2016), pp. 104–22.

11 Helen Fair and Roy Walmsley, *World Prison Population List, 13th Edition* (ICPR, 2022), https://www.prisonstudies.org/sites/

default/files/resources/downloads/world_prison_population_
list_13th_edition.pdf

12   John Pratt, 'Scandinavian exceptionalism in an era of penal excess:
      Part I: The nature and roots of Scandinavian exceptionalism', *The
      British Journal of Criminology* 48 (2008), pp. 119–37; John Pratt,
      'Scandinavian exceptionalism in an era of penal excess: Part II:
      does Scandinavian exceptionalism have a future?', *The British
      Journal of Criminology* 48 (2008), pp. 275–92; Thomas Ugelvik
      and Dorina Damsa, 'The pains of crimmigration imprisonment:
      Perspectives from a Norwegian all-foreign prison', *The British
      Journal of Criminology* 58 (2018), pp. 1025–43.

13   The opposing ideas about human nature are often discussed with
      reference to the political philosophies described in Thomas Hobbes,
      Leviathan, edited by C.B. Macpherson (Penguin, 1985), and Jean-
      Jacques Rousseau, *The Social Contract* (Penguin, 2004).

14   Thomas Mathiesen, *Prison on Trial* (Waterside Press, 2006).

15   Michelle Alexander, *The New Jim Crow: Mass Incarceration in the
      Age of Colorblindness* (New Press, 2010).

16   Joe Sim, *Punishment and Prisons: Power and the Carceral State*
      (Sage Publications, 2009). See also, Vincent Ruggiero, *Penal
      Abolitionism* (Oxford University Press, 2010).

17   Roy Walmsley, *World Female Imprisonment List* (4th edition,
      ICPR, 2017), https://www.prisonstudies.org/news/world-female-
      imprisonment-list-fourth-edition

Chapter 2

1   Pat Carlen and Anne Worrall, *Analysing Women's Imprisonment*
      (2nd edition, Routledge, 2012), p. 5.

2   Many accomplished accounts are available for anyone who is
      interested in learning more. For mainly US and UK prisons, see
      Norval Morris and David J. Rothman (eds), *The Oxford History of
      the Prison: The Practice of Punishment in Western Society* (Oxford
      University Press, 1995). For British prisons, see Harry Potter,
      *Shades of the Prison House: A History of Incarceration in the
      British Isles* (The Boydell Press, 2019). For US prisons, see Mary
      Bosworth, *Explaining US Imprisonment* (Sage Publications, 2010).
      For a concise review of global prison history, see Mary Gibson,
      'Global perspectives on the birth of the prison', *The American
      Historical Review* 116 (2011), pp. 1040–63. For an incisive
      analysis of the history of women's imprisonment, see Carlen and
      Worrall, *Analysing Women's Imprisonment*, chapter 1.

NOTES

3   For a fascinating account of American prisons, racial politics and the social order in US before the Civil War, see Austin Reed, *The Life and the Adventures of a Haunted Convict*, edited by Caleb Smith (Random House, *c.* 1858/2016).

4   Edward M. Peters, 'Prison before the prison: The ancient and medieval worlds', in Morris and Rothman, *The Oxford History of the Prison: The Practice of Punishment in Western Society*.

5   Peters, 'Prison before the prison: The ancient and medieval worlds'.

6   John Howard, *The State of the Prisons in England and Wales: With Preliminary Observations, and an Account of Some Foreign Prisons and Hospitals* (William Eyres, 1777).

7   Cited by Tawny Paul, 'The scale of incarceration: Debt and the middling sort', in *The Poverty of Disaster: Debt and Insecurity in Eighteenth-Century Britain*, Cambridge Studies in Early Modern British History (Cambridge University Press, 2019), pp. 31–66 [pp. 33–4].

8   Paul, 'The scale of incarceration: Debt and the middling sort', p. 34.

9   Paul, 'The scale of incarceration: Debt and the middling sort', p. 34.

10   Charles Dickens, 'Philadelphia, and its solitary prison', in *American Notes for General Circulation* (Cambridge Library Collection – North American History, Cambridge University Press, 2009), pp. 231–68 [p. 238].

11   Potter, *Shades of the Prison House: A History of Incarceration in the British Isles*.

12   HMIP, *Report on an Unannounced Inspection of HMP Pentonville, 4–5 and 11–14 July 2022* (HMIP, 2022), https://www.justiceinspectorates.gov.uk/hmiprisons/wp-content/uploads/sites/4/2022/10/Pentonville-web-2022.pdf

13   E.g. Jeremy Bentham, *An Introduction to the Principles of Morals and Legislation* (Clarendon Press, 1789/1907).

14   Michael Ignatieff, 'State, civil society, and total institutions: A critique of recent social histories of punishment', in *Crime and Justice* 3 (1981), pp. 153–92 [p. 156].

15   Carlen and Worrall, *Analysing Women's Imprisonment*, p. 6.

16   Carlen and Worrall, *Analysing Women's Imprisonment*, p. 6.

17   V. Camille Westmont, 'Dark heritage in the New South: Remembering convict leasing in Southern Middle Tennessee through community archaeology', *International Journal of Historical Archaeology* 26 (2022), pp. 1–21 [p. 3].

18   Gibson, 'Global perspectives on the birth of the prison', p. 1044.

19   Michel Foucault, *Discipline and Punish: The Birth of the Prison* (Pantheon, 1977).

20   Foucault, *Discipline and Punish*, p. 3.

21   Foucault, *Discipline and Punish*, p. 16.

22   Foucault, *Discipline and Punish*, pp. 302–3.

23   Carlen and Worrall, *Analysing Women's Imprisonment*, p. 6.

24   Dr Cartwright, 'Diseases and peculiarities of the Negro race', *DeBow's Review* XI (1851), PBS, Africans in America, https://www.pbs.org/wgbh/aia/part4/4h3106t.html

25   John S. Haller Jr., 'The Negro and the Southern physician: A study of medical and racial attitudes 1800–1860', in *Medical History* 16 (1972), pp. 238–53.

26   E.g. Georg Rusche and Otto Kirchheimer, *Punishment and Social Structure* (Columbia University Press, 1939); Dario Melossi, Massimo Pavarini and Glynis Cousin (translator), *The Prison and the Factory: Origins of the Penitentiary System* (Barnes and Noble Books, 1981).

27   David Garland, *Culture of Control: Crime and Social Order in Contemporary Society* (Oxford University Press, 2001).

28   Garland, *Culture of Control*, p. 202.

29   Carlen and Worrall, *Analysing Women's Imprisonment*, p. 122.

30   John M. Moore, 'Penal reform: A history of failure', in *Criminal Justice Matters* 77 (2009), pp. 12–13 [p. 13] https://www.tandfonline.com/doi/full/10.1080/09627250903139264

31   Ignatieff, 'State, civil society, and total institutions: A critique of recent social histories of punishment', p. 157.

32   Lucia Zedner, 'Wayward sister: The prison for women', in Norval Morris and David J. Rothman (eds), *Oxford History of the Prison: The Practice of Punishment in Western Society* (Oxford University Press, 1997), pp. 329–61.

33   Florence Bernault, 'The politics of enclosure in colonial and post-colonial Africa', in Florence Bernault (ed) *The History of Prison and Confinement in Africa* (Heinemann, 2003), pp. 1–53.

34   Lucia Zedner, 'Women, crime, and penal responses: A historical account', in *Crime and Justice* 14 (1991), pp. 307–62 [p. 308].

35   Dickens, 'Philadelphia, and Its solitary prison', p. 251.

36   See Carlen and Worrall, *Analysing Women's Imprisonment*, p. 12.

37   Zedner, 'Wayward sister: The prison for women', p. 303.

38 A prominent example of this in the UK context is the case of child murderer Myra Hindley, see Nina Wilde, *The Monstering of Myra Hindley* (Waterside Press, 2016).

39 Zedner, 'Wayward sister: The prison for women', p. 318.

40 Davis, *Are Prisons Obsolete?*, p. 72.

41 Zedner, 'Women, crime, and penal responses: A historical account', p. 308.

42 Zedner, 'Wayward sister: The prison for women', p. 318.

43 See Carlen and Worrall, *Analysing Women's Imprisonment*, p. 2.

44 Rashida Manjoo, *Women and Detention* (United Nations Office of the High Commissioner for Human Rights (UNOHCHR), 2014), https://www.ohchr.org/sites/default/files/Documents/Issues/Women/WRGS/OnePagers/Women_and_Detention.pdf; UNOHCHR Working Group on the issue of discrimination against women in law and in practice, *Adultery as a Criminal Offence Violates Women's Rights* (UNOHCHR, 2012), https://www.ohchr.org/sites/default/files/Documents/Issues/Women/WG/AdulteryasaCriminalOffenceViolatesWomenHR.pdf

45 Sanhita Ambast, Hazal Atay and Antonella Lavelanet, 'A global review of penalties for abortion-related offences in 182 countries', in *British Medical Journal Global Health* 8 (e010405, 2023).

46 Helen Fair and Roy Walmsley, *World Female Imprisonment List* (Institute for Crime and Justice Policy Research, 2022), https://www.prisonstudies.org/sites/default/files/resources/downloads/world_female_imprisonment_list_5th_edition.pdf

47 Ministry of Justice (MoJ), *Prison Population Projections 2020 to 2026, England and Wales* (MoJ, 2020), p. 12, https://assets.publishing.service.gov.uk/government/uploads/system/uploads/attachment_data/file/938571/Prison_Population_Projections_2020_to_2026.pdf

48 See Carlen and Worrall, *Analysing Women's Imprisonment*.

Chapter 3

1 See Carlen and Worrall, *Analysing Women's Imprisonment*, p. 5.

2 Jeremy Sarkin, 'Prisons in Africa: An evaluation from a human rights perspective', *Sur International Journal on Human Rights* 4 (2008), pp. 22–49 [p. 24].

3 Bernault, 'The politics of enclosure in colonial and post-colonial Africa', p. 5.

4 Sarkin, 'Prisons in Africa'.

5   Bernault, 'The politics of enclosure in colonial and post-colonial Africa', p. 3.

6   Daniel Branch, 'Imprisonment and colonialism in Kenya, c. 1930–1952: Escaping the carceral archipelago', *The International Journal of African Historical Studies* 38 (2005), pp. 239–65 [p. 246].

7   Branch, 'Imprisonment and colonialism in Kenya, c. 1930–1952', p. 244.

8   Gibson, 'Global perspectives on the birth of the prison', p. 1053.

9   Ali Rattansi, *Racism: A Very Short Introduction* (Oxford University Press, 2020).

10 Bernault, 'The politics of enclosure in colonial and post-colonial Africa', p. 3.

11 Katharine Gerbner, *Christian Slavery: Conversion and Race in the Protestant Atlantic World* (University of Pennsylvania Press, 2018), p. 74.

12 Peter Zinoman, *The Colonial Bastille: A History of Imprisonment in Vietnam, 1862–1940* (University of California Press, 2001), p. 33.

13 Zinoman, *The Colonial Bastille*, p. 1.

14 Fair and Walmsley, *World Prison Population List*, 2022.

15 Sarkin, 'Prisons in Africa'.

16 Garland, *Culture of Control*, p. 202.

17 Sarkin, 'Prisons in Africa'.

18 United Nations Office on Drugs and Crime (UNODC), *The United Nations Standard Minimum Rules for the Treatment of Prisoners (the Nelson Mandela Rules)* (United Nations, 2015), https://www.unodc.org/documents/justice-and-prison-reform/Nelson_Mandela_Rules-E-ebook.pdf

19 Carlos Aguirre, 'Prisons and prisoners in modernising Latin America (1800–1940)', in Dikötter and Brown (eds), *Cultures of Confinement: A History of the Prison in Africa, Asia, and Latin America* (Cornell University Press, 2007), pp. 14–54 [p. 19].

20 Daniel V. Botsman, *Punishment and Power in the Making of Modern Japan* (Princeton University Press, 2004).

21 Botsman, *Punishment and Power in the Making of Modern Japan*, p. 116.

22 Botsman, *Punishment and Power in the Making of Modern Japan*, p. 165.

23 Botsman, *Punishment and Power in the Making of Modern Japan*, p. 166.

24   Botsman, *Punishment and Power in the Making of Modern Japan*,
     p. 124–5.
25   Botsman, *Punishment and Power in the Making of Modern Japan*,
     p. 188.
26   World Prison Brief: Japan, https://www.prisonstudies.org/country/
     japan
27   World Prison Brief, England and Wales, https://www.prisonstudies.
     org/country/united-kingdom-england-wales; World Prison Brief,
     Norway, https://www.prisonstudies.org/country/norway; World
     Prison Brief, Finland, https://www.prisonstudies.org/country/finland
28   Andrew Coyle, *Prisons of the World* (Bristol University Press,
     2021).
29   Saki Kato, 'Probation in Japan: Engaging the community', *Irish
     Probation Journal* 15 (2018), pp. 114–136; Andrew Watson,
     'Probation in Japan: Strengths and challenges and likely new tasks',
     European Journal of Probation 10 (2018), pp. 160–77.
30   Laura Piacentini, *Surviving Russian Prisons: Punishment, Economy
     and Politics in Transition* (Willan, 2004).
31   Laura Piacentini, *Russian Prisons: Bringing a Riddle Out of
     Hiding*, e-Sharp (2009), pp. 74–98 [80].
32   Piacentini, *Surviving Russian Prisons*, p. xiii.
33   Coyle, *Prisons of the World*, p. 56.
34   Coyle, *Prisons of the World*, p. 57.
35   Piacentini, *Russian Prisons*.
36   Coyle, *Prisons of the World*, p. 58.
37   Jan Strzelecki, *Russia Behind Bars: The Peculiarities of the Russian
     Prison System*, OSW (Centre for Eastern Studies) Commentary
     293 (2019), https://www.osw.waw.pl/sites/default/files/
     commentary_293_0.pdf; Coyle, *Prisons of the World*; Piacentini,
     Surviving Russian Prisons.
38   CPT, *Report to the Russian Government on the visit to the
     Russian Federation carried out by the European Committee for
     the Prevention of Torture and Inhuman or Degrading Treatment
     or Punishment from 21 May to 4 June 2012* (CPT, 2013), https://
     rm.coe.int/1680697bd6
39   Strzelecki, *Russia Behind Bars*.
40   Emma Kaufman and Mary Bosworth, 'The prison and national
     identity: Citizenship, punishment and the sovereign state', in D.
     Scott (ed.) *Why Prison?* (Cambridge University Press, 2013),
     p. 187.

41 Stephen Castles and Mark J. Miller, *The Age of Migration: International Population Movements in the Modern World* (4th edition, Palgrave Macmillan, 2009).

42 Benedict Anderson, *Imagined Communities* (Verso, 1991).

43 Castles and Miller, *The Age of Migration*, p. 115.

44 Hindpal Singh Bhui, 'The place of "race" in immigration control and the detention of foreign nationals', *Criminology and Criminal Justice* 16 (2016), pp. 267–85.

45 See Ana Aliverti, *Crimes of Mobility: Criminal Law and the Regulation of Immigration* (Routledge, 2013).

46 Hindpal Singh Bhui, 'Humanising immigration control and detention', in Katja Franko Aas and Mary Bosworth (eds) *Borders of Punishment: Migration, Citizenship, and Social Exclusion* (Oxford University Press, 2013).

47 Emma Kaufman, *Punish and Expel: Border Control, Nationalism, and the New Purpose of the Prison* (Oxford Academic, 2015), p. 14.

48 Kaufman, *Punish and Expel*, p. 208.

49 All case studies in the book are anonymized. All the events reported in them happened, but I have changed names and, in one case, I have combined two stories to avoid any risk of identification.

Chapter 4

1 Barack Obama, 'Remarks by the President at the NAACP Conference', Pennsylvania Convention Center, Philadelphia, Pennsylvania, 14 July 2015, https://obamawhitehouse.archives.gov/the-press-office/2015/07/14/remarks-president-naacp-conference

2 For example, in England and Wales, the prison population has doubled since 1993 and is predicted to jump from around 84,000 in March 2023 to as high as 106,300 by March 2027. See Ministry of Justice (MoJ), *Story of the Prison Population 1993–2020 England and Wales* (MoJ, 2020), https://assets.publishing.service.gov.uk/media/5f9959aae90e0740770c85af/Story_of_the_Prison_Population_1993-2020.pdf; MoJ, *Prison Population Projections 2022 to 2027, England and Wales* (MoJ, 2023), https://assets.publishing.service.gov.uk/government/uploads/system/uploads/attachment_data/file/1138135/Prison_Population_Projections_2022_to_2027.pdf

3 World Prison Brief, USA (data accessed 20 April 2023), https://www.prisonstudies.org/country/united-states-america

4   Loïc Wacquant, 'From slavery to mass incarceration', *New Left Review* 13 (2002), pp. 41–60.

5   Julian V. Roberts, Loretta J. Stalans, David Indemaur and Mike Hough, *Penal Populism and Public Opinion: Lessons from Five Countries* (Oxford University Press, 2003), p. 24.

6   David Garland, 'What is penal populism? Public opinion, expert knowledge, and penal policy-formation in democratic societies', in Alison Liebling, Joanna Shapland, Richard Sparks, and Justice Tankebe (eds) *Crime, Justice, and Social Order: Essays in Honour of A.E. Bottoms* (Oxford Academic, 2022), p. 252.

7   Richard Nixon, 'Special Message to the Congress on Drug Abuse Prevention and Control', 17 June 1971, American Presidency Project, https://www.presidency.ucsb.edu/documents/special-message-the-congress-drug-abuse-prevention-and-control

8   National Research Council, *The Growth of Incarceration in the United States: Exploring Causes and Consequences* (The National Academies Press, 2014), p. 119.

9   Dan Baum, 'Legalize it all: How to win the war on drugs', *Harpers Magazine*, April 2016, https://harpers.org/archive/2016/04/legalize-it-all/

10   Harry R. Haldeman, *The Haldeman Diaries: Inside the Nixon White House* (G.P. Putnam's Sons, 1994), p. 53, cited in National Research Council, *The Growth of Incarceration in the United States*, p. 116.

11   Ashley Nellis, *Mass Incarceration Trends*, The Sentencing Project, 25 January 2023, p. 5, https://www.sentencingproject.org/reports/mass-incarceration-trends/ ; see also, Jamila Hodge and Nazish Dholakia, 'fifty years ago today, President Nixon declared the war on drugs', Vera Institute for Justice, 17 June 2021, https://www.vera.org/news/fifty-years-ago-today-president-nixon-declared-the-war-on-drugs

12   National Research Council, *The Growth of Incarceration in the United States*, pp. 119–20.

13   Nellis, *Mass Incarceration Trends*, p. 5.

14   Frost and Clear, 'Theories of mass incarceration', p. 105.

15   Nazgol Ghandoosh, *Ending 50 Years of Mass Incarceration: Urgent Reform Needed to Protect Future Generations*, The Sentencing Project, 8 February 2023, https://www.sentencingproject.org/policy-brief/ending-50-years-of-mass-incarceration-urgent-reform-needed-to-protect-future-generations/

16   Nazish Dholakia, 'Biden's cannabis pardons are one small step to ending the "war on drugs." Much more is needed', Vera Institute for Justice, 13 October 2022, https://www.vera.org/news/bidens-cannabis-pardons-one-small-step-to-ending-war-on-drugs-much-more-needed

17   Frost and Clear, 'Theories of mass incarceration'.

18   For example, see Nicola Archer, Megan Butler, Georgia Avukatu and Emma Williams Savanta (2022) *Public Knowledge of and Confidence in the Criminal Justice System and Sentencing: 2022 Research*, https://www.sentencingcouncil.org.uk/wp-content/uploads/2022-12-12-P019988-Sentencing-Council_Perceptions_Report_v14_FINAL.pdf; Nicola Marsh, Emma McKay, Clara Pelly and Simon Cereda (2019) *Public Knowledge of and Confidence in the Criminal Justice System and Sentencing a Report for the Sentencing Council*, ComRes, https://www.sentencingcouncil.org.uk/wp-content/uploads/Public-Knowledge-of-and-Confidence-in-the-Criminal-Justice-System-and-Sentencing.pdf; *House of Commons Justice Committee Survey*, March 2023, https://committees.parliament.uk/writtenevidence/119614/default/

19   National Research Council, *The Growth of Incarceration in the United States*, p. 340.

20   Wille Horton 1988 Attack Ad, https://www.youtube.com/watch?v=Io9KMSSEZ0Y&t=1s

21   Bill Keller, quoted in *The Takeaway*, 'The campaign ad that reshaped criminal justice', 18 May 2015, https://www.wnycstudios.org/podcasts/takeaway/segments/crime-reshaped-criminal-justice

22   Ruth Delaney, Ram Subramanian, Alison Shames and Nicholas Turner, 'American history, race and prison', Vera Institute for Justice website, undated, https://www.vera.org/reimagining-prison-web-report/american-history-race-and-prison

23   Mike Wessler, 'Updated charts provide insights on racial disparities, correctional control, jail suicides, and more', Prison Policy Initiative, 19 May 2022, https://www.prisonpolicy.org/blog/2022/05/19/updated_charts/

24   Ashley Nellis, *The Color of Justice: Racial and Ethnic Disparity in State Prisons*, The Sentencing Project, 13 October 2021, p. 4, https://www.sentencingproject.org/app/uploads/2022/08/The-Color-of-Justice-Racial-and-Ethnic-Disparity-in-State-Prisons.pdf

25   Joshua M. Price, *Prison and Social Death* (Rutgers University Press, 2015).

26   For example, see French sociologist Loïc Wacquant's identification of the four institutions designed to confine and control African-Americans as: chattel slavery, 'Jim Crow', the urban ghetto and the prison: Loïc Wacquant, 'The new "peculiar institution": On the prison as surrogate ghetto', *Theoretical Criminology* 4 (2000), pp. 377–89.

27   Michelle Alexander, *The New Jim Crow: Mass Incarceration in the Age of Colorblindness* (New Press, 2010), p. 207.

28   Albert Woodfox, *Solitary* (Text Publishing, 2019), p. 22.

29   John Gramlich, 'Black imprisonment rate in the U.S. has fallen by a third since 2006', Pew Research Center website, 6 May 2020, https://www.pewresearch.org/fact-tank/2020/05/06/share-of-black-white-hispanic-americans-in-prison-2018-vs-2006/ (The data on race excludes remands, those held in US local prisons, or with sentences shorter than a year.)

30   David Northrup, 'Overseas movements of slaves and indentured workers', in David Eltis, Stanley L. Engerman, Seymour Drescher and David Richardson (eds), *The Cambridge World History of Slavery, Vol 4* (Cambridge University Press, 2017), pp. 49–70.

31   Michael Tonry, 'Why crime rates are falling throughout the Western world', *Crime and Justice* 43 (2014), pp. 1–63 [p. 3].

32   National Research Council, *The Growth of Incarceration in the United States*, p. 4.

33   Don Stemen, *The Prison Paradox: More Incarceration Will Not Make Us Safer* (Vera Institute, 2017), pp. 1–2, https://www.vera.org/downloads/publications/for-the-record-prison-paradox_02.pdf

34   For example, see Patrick Bayer, Randi Hjalmarsson and David Pozen, 'Building criminal capital behind bars: peer effects in juvenile corrections', *The Quarterly Journal of Economics* 124 (2009), pp. 105–47.

35   Frost and Clear, 'Theories of mass incarceration', p. 109.

36   Todd Clear, *Imprisoning Communities: How Mass Incarceration Makes Disadvantaged Neighborhoods Worse* (Oxford University Press, 2009). See also, Todd Clear, 'The effects of high imprisonment rates on communities', *Crime and Justice* 37 (2008), pp. 97–132; and Tonry, 'Why crime rates are falling throughout the Western world', p. 3.

37   FWD.US, Every Second: The Impact of the Incarceration Crisis on America's Families (FWD.US, 2018).

38   House of Commons Justice Committee, *Cutting Crime: the Case for Justice Reinvestment*, First Report of Session 2009–10 (HoC,

2011), https://publications.parliament.uk/pa/cm200910/cmselect/
cmjust/94/94i.pdf

39 See Luiz Dal Santo, 'Brazilian prisons in times of mass
incarceration: Ambivalent transformations', *The Howard Journal
of Crime and Justice* 61 (2022), pp. 502–18, and Sacha Darke,
Conviviality and Survival: Co-producing Brazilian Prison Order
(Springer, 2018).

40 Leonardo Coutinho, 'The evolution of the most lethal criminal
organization in Brazil—the PCC', in *Prism* 8 (2019), pp. 56–67
[p. 65], https://ndupress.ndu.edu/PRISM/PRISM-8-1/

41 Sacha Darke and Maria Lúcia Karam, 'Latin American prisons',
in Yvonne Jewkes, Jamie Bennett and Ben Crewe (eds) *Handbook
on Prisons* (2nd edition, Routledge, 2016), cited by Dal Santo,
'Brazilian prisons in times of mass incarceration', p. 509.

42 Sacha Darke, 'Managing without guards in a Brazilian police
lockup', *Focaal* 68 (2014), pp. 55–67 [p. 64], cited by Dal Santo,
'Brazilian prisons in times of mass incarceration', p. 509.

43 Tapio Lappi-Seppälä, 'The fall of the Finnish prison population',
*Journal of Scandinavian Studies in Criminology and Crime
Prevention* 1 (2000), pp. 27–40.

44 Patrik Törnudd, 'Fifteen years of decreasing prisoner rates in
Finland', in National Research Institute of Legal Policy, *Research
Communication* 8 (1993), p. 13. Quoted by Lappi-Seppälä, 'The
fall of the Finnish prison population', p. 37 [no English translation
of original book].

45 Lappi-Seppälä, 'The fall of the Finnish prison population', p. 38.

46 Lappi-Seppälä, 'The fall of the Finnish prison population', p. 37.

47 Lappi-Seppälä, 'The fall of the Finnish prison population', p. 29.

48 David Wilson, *Pain and Retribution: A Short History of British
Prisons, 1066 to the Present* (Reaktion Books, 2014), pp. 88–9.

Chapter 5

1 Aleksandr Solzhenitsyn, *The Gulag Archipelago (1918–1956)*,
translated by Thomas P. Whitney and Harry Willetts (Harvill Press,
2003), p. 75.

2 Donald Macintyre, 'Major on crime: "Condemn more, understand
less"', in *The Independent*, 21 February 1993, https://www.
independent.co.uk/news/major-on-crime-condemn-more-
understand-less-1474470.html

3 Peter Hitchens, *A Brief History of Crime* (Atlantic Books, 2003).

4   Penal Reform International and Thailand Institute of Justice, *Global Prison Trends 2022*, https://cdn.penalreform.org/wp-content/uploads/2022/05/GPT2022.pdf; Penal Reform International and Thailand Institute of Justice, *Global Prison Trends 2021*, https://cdn.penalreform.org/wp-content/uploads/2021/05/Global-prison-trends-2021.pdf

5   Daniel P. Mears and Joshua C. Cochran, 'Who goes to prison?' in John Wooldredge and Paula Smith, *The Oxford Handbook of Prisons and Imprisonment* (Oxford University Press, 2018), pp. 29–52 [p. 50].

6   Penal Reform International and Thailand Institute of Justice, *Global Prison Trends 2022*, p. 12.

7   Penal Reform International and Thailand Institute of Justice, *Global Prison Trends 2022*.

8   See, for example, Rhona Epstein, 'It is more urgent than ever that we end the criminalisation of poverty', *British Medical Journal* blog, 21 May 2021, https://blogs.bmj.com/bmj/2021/05/21/it-is-more-urgent-than-ever-that-we-end-the-criminalisation-of-poverty/; And an insightful talk by Epstein, 'Addiction – stigma, inequities and punishment', 4 October 2022, https://www.chadresearch.co.uk/webinar-addiction-stigma-inequities-and-punishment/?utm_source=rss&utm_medium=rss&utm_campaign=webinar-addiction-stigma-inequities-and-punishment

9   'Decriminalising rough sleeping and begging: Calls for repealing the Vagrancy Act 1824', House of Commons Library, 17 April 2020, https://lordslibrary.parliament.uk/decriminalising-rough-sleeping-and-begging-calls-for-repealing-the-vagrancy-act-1824/

10   'Policy Paper: Repeal of the Vagrancy Act 1824: Police, Crime, Sentencing and Courts Act 2022 Factsheet', UK Government website, https://www.gov.uk/government/publications/police-crime-sentencing-and-courts-bill-2021-factsheets/repeal-of-the-vagrancy-act-1824-police-crime-sentencing-and-courts-act-2022-factsheet

11   Chris Atkins, *A Bit of a Stretch: The Diaries of a Prisoner* (Atlantic Books, 2020), p. 30.

12   HMI Prisons (2015) *Life in Prison: The First 24 Hours in Prison*, p. 12, https://www.justiceinspectorates.gov.uk/hmiprisons/wp-content/uploads/sites/4/2015/11/HMIP-First-24-hours-findings-paper-web-2015.pdf

13   Seena Fazel and Katharina Seewald, 'Severe mental illness in 33,588 prisoners worldwide: systematic review and meta-regression analysis', *The British Journal of Psychiatry* 200 (2012), pp. 364–73.

14 Penal Reform International and Thailand Institute of Justice, *Global Prison Trends 2022*.

15 Prison Policy Initiative, 'Policies and practices surrounding mental health' (undated), https://www.prisonpolicy.org/research/mental_health/

16 Treatment Advocacy Centre, *The Treatment of Persons with Mental Illness in Prisons and Jails: A State Survey* (2014), https://www.treatmentadvocacycenter.org/storage/documents/treatment-behind-bars/treatment-behind-bars.pdf

17 National Audit Office, 'Mental Health in Prisons', Press Release, 29 June 2017, https://www.nao.org.uk/reports/mental-health-in-prisons/#:~:text=Government%20does%20not%20know%20how,it%20is%20achieving%20its%20objectives

18 Nichola Tyler, Helen L. Miles, Bessey Karadag and Gemma Rogers, 'An updated picture of the mental health needs of male and female prisoners in the UK: Prevalence, comorbidity, and gender differences', *Social Psychiatry and Psychiatric Epidemiology* 54 (2019), pp. 1143–52.

19 National Audit Office, *Mental Health in Prisons* (NAO, 2017); Nivedita Rebbapragada, Vivek Furtado and George William Hawker-Bond, 'Prevalence of mental disorders in prisons in the UK: A systematic review and meta-analysis', *British Journal of Psychiatry Open* 7 (S1) (2021), pp. S283–4; Tyler et al, 'An updated picture of the mental health needs of male and female prisoners in the UK'.

20 Angela Davis, 'Masked racism: reflections on the prison industrial complex', *ColorLines Magazine* (Fall 1998), https://colorlines.com/article/masked-racism-reflections-prison-industrial-complex/

21 Seena Fazel, Taanvi Ramesh and Keith Hawton, 'Suicide in prisons: An international study of prevalence and contributory factors', *Lancet Psychiatry* 4 (2017), pp. 946–52.

22 Daniel Pratt, Mary Piper, Louis Appleby, Roger Webb and Jenny Shaw, 'Suicide in recently released prisoners: A population-based cohort study', *Lancet* 368 (2006), pp. 119–23; for the US context, see Ingrid A. Binswanger, Marc F. Stern, Richard A. Deyo, Patrick J. Heagerty, Allen Cheadle, Joann G. Elmore and Thomas D. Koepsell, 'Release from prison – a high risk of death for former inmates', *New England Journal of Medicine* 356 (2007), pp. 157–65; for a brief summary of research, see Fazel and Seewald, 'Severe mental illness in 33,588 prisoners worldwide', p. 364.

23 See, for example, the excellent MIND website description of racial trauma, 'Racism and mental health', https://www.mind.org.uk/information-support/tips-for-everyday-living/racism-and-mental-health/#RacialTrauma

24 Claire Bodkin, Lucie Pivnick, Susan J. Bondy, Carolyn Ziegler, Ruth Elwood Martin, Carey Jernigan and Fiona Kouyoumdjian, 'History of childhood abuse in populations incarcerated in Canada: A systematic review and meta-analysis', *American Journal of Public Health* 109 (2019), pp. e1–e11.

25 Prison Reform Trust, *Bromley Briefings Prison Factfile: Winter 2022* (PRT, 2022), https://prisonreformtrust.org.uk/wp-content/uploads/2022/02/Winter-2022-Factfile.pdf

26 For details, see Hope Kent and Huw Williams, *Traumatic Brain Injury* (HM Inspectorate of Probation, 2021), p. 7, https://www.justiceinspectorates.gov.uk/hmiprobation/wp-content/uploads/sites/5/2021/08/Academic-Insights-Kent-and-Williams-LL-v2.0-RMdocx.pdf

27 Jude Kelman, Rachael Gribble, Joel Harvey, Laura Palmer and Deirdre MacManus, 'How does a history of trauma affect the experience of imprisonment for individuals in women's prisons: a qualitative exploration', *Women and Criminal Justice*, Open Access Online Journal (2022), p. 15, https://www.tandfonline.com/doi/epdf/10.1080/08974454.2022.2071376?needAccess=true&role=button; see also, Ben Crewe, Susie Hulley and Serena Wright, 'The gendered pains of life imprisonment', in *British Journal of Criminology* 57 (2017), 1359–78 [pp. 1363–4].

28 See 'One Small Thing' website, https://onesmallthing.org.uk/

29 Katherine M. Auty, Alison Liebling, Anna Schliehe and Ben Crewe, 'What is trauma-informed practice? Towards operationalisation of the concept in two prisons for women', *Criminology and Criminal Justice* 23(5) (2023), 716–38.

30 Dylan S. Cooper, Disha Uppal, Kirsten S. Railey, Amy Blank Wilson, Katie Maras, Emily Zimmerman et al, 'Policy gaps and opportunities: A systematic review of autism spectrum disorder and criminal justice intersections', *Autism* 26 (2022), pp. 1014–31. For examples of such units, see Criminal Justice Inspectorates, *Neurodiversity in the Criminal Justice System: A Review of Evidence* (CJ Inspectorates, 2021), https://www.justiceinspectorates.gov.uk/cjji/inspections/neurodiversity-in-the-criminal-justice-system-a-review-of-evidence/

31 Criminal Justice Inspectorates, *Neurodiversity in the Criminal Justice System*, p. 20.

32 Kent and Williams, *Traumatic Brain Injury*, p. 4.

33 Kent and Williams, *Traumatic Brain Injury*.

34 Kent and Williams, *Traumatic Brain Injury*, p. 7.

35 Centers for Disease Control and Prevention, 'Traumatic brain injury in prisons and jails: An unrecognized problem' (undated), https://www.cdc.gov/traumaticbraininjury/pdf/Prisoner_TBI_Prof-a.pdf

36 Criminal Justice Inspectorates, *Neurodiversity in the Criminal Justice System*, p. 20.

37 Tom M. McMillan, Hira Aslam, Eimear Crowe, Eleanor Seddon and Sarah J. E. Barry, 'Associations between significant head injury and persisting disability and violent crime in women in prison in Scotland, UK: A cross-sectional study', *Lancet Psychiatry* 8 (2021), pp. 512–20.

38 Ivan Pitman, Claire Haddlesey, Sara D. S. Ramos, Michael Oddy and Deborah Fortescue, 'The association between neuropsychological performance and self-reported traumatic brain injury in a sample of adult male prisoners in the UK', *Neuropsychological Rehabilitation* 25 (2015), pp. 763–79.

39 The Disabilities Trust, *Making the Link: Female Offending and Brain Injury* (The Barrow Cadbury Trust, 2019), https://barrowcadbury.org.uk/wp-content/uploads/2019/01/Making-the-Link-Female-Offending-and-Brain-Injury-low-resolution.pdf

40 Disabilities Trust Foundation, *Brain Injury Linkworker Service* (Disabilities Trust, 2016), https://brainkind.org/wp-content/uploads/2023/09/Foundation-Outcome-Report_dft4-1.pdf

41 Daniel S. Nagin, 'Deterrence: A review of the evidence by a criminologist for economists', *Annual Review of Economics* 5 (2013), pp. 83–105.

42 Nagin, 'Deterrence: A review of the evidence by a criminologist for economists'.

43 David Ramsbotham, *Prisongate: The Shocking State of Britain's Prisons and the Need for Visionary Change* (Simon & Schuster UK Ltd, 2003).

44 Fergus McNeill, 'Rehabilitation, corrections and society', Distinguished Scholar address to the ICPA conference, *Advancing Corrections Journal*, Edition 5, 2018, p. 17, http://eprints.gla.ac.uk/159625/7/159625.pdf

45 McNeill, 'Rehabilitation, corrections and society', p. 18.

Chapter 6

1 For a detailed and nuanced account of the impact on staff of working in prisons, see South, *Behind These Doors*.

2 Anonymous, *The Secret Prisoner: Diary of a Prisoner* (independently published, 2021), p. 22.

3 Atkins, *A Bit of a Stretch*, p. 30.

4 See 'Prison Project: Little Scandinavia (Extended Trailer)', https://www.youtube.com/watch?v=gTC1KI0STIY

5 Shaoling Zhong, Morwenna Senior, Rongqin Yu, Amanda Perry, Keith Hawton, Jenny Shaw and Seena Fazel, 'Risk factors for suicide in prisons: a systematic review and meta-analysis', *Lancet Public Health* (2021), pp. e164–74.

6 PPO news release, 20 February 2018, https://www.ppo.gov.uk/news/self-inflicted-death-of-18-year-old-lithuanian-man-at-hmp-wandsworth-an-appalling-case-says-the-prisons-and-probation-ombudsman/ (full report: Prisons and Probation Ombudsman for England and Wales, *Independent Investigation into the Death of Mr Osvaldas Pagirys a Prisoner at HMP Wandsworth on 14 November 2016* (PPO, 2017)).

7 Atkins, *A Bit of a Stretch*, p. 163.

8 Jerry Metcalf, 'Life inside: A day in the life of a prisoner', The Marshall Project, 7 December 2018, https://www.themarshallproject.org/2018/07/12/a-day-in-the-life-of-a-prisoner

9 Albert Woodfox, *Solitary: Unbroken by Four Decades in Solitary Confinement. My Story of Transformation and Hope* (Text Publishing Company, 2019), p. 42.

10 Anonymous, *The Secret Prisoner*, p. 21.

11 See CPT (2023) *Report to the Government of the Netherlands on the Periodic Visit to the Kingdom of the Netherlands Carried Out by the European Committee for the Prevention of Torture and Inhuman or Degrading Treatment or Punishment (CPT) from 10 to 25 May 2022*, https://rm.coe.int/1680abb4b5

12 Assata Shakur, *Assata: An Autobiography* (Lawrence Hill and Co, 1987), pp. 83–4, quoted in Davis, *Are Prisons Obsolete?*, p. 63.

13 Woodfox, *Solitary*, p. 162.

14 Jason Warr, '"Always gotta be two mans": Lifers, risk, rehabilitation, and narrative labour', in *Punishment & Society* 22 (2020), pp. 28–47 [p. 28].

15 PRT, *Long-term Prisoners: The Facts, England and Wales* (PRT, 2021), https://prisonreformtrust.org.uk/wp-content/uploads/2021/10/Long-term-prisoners_the-facts_2021.pdf

16 Ben Crewe, 'Depth, weight, tightness: Revisiting the pains of imprisonment', in *Punishment & Society* 13 (2011), pp. 509–29 [p. 516].

17 Warr, '"Always gotta be two mans"', p. 28.

18 HMI Prisons, *The Experiences of Adult Black Male Prisoners and Black Prison Staff* (HMIP, 2022).

19 Gresham Sykes, *The Society of Captives* (Princeton University Press, 1958).

20 Lord Justice Woolf, *Prison Disturbances, April 1990*, Cm. 1456 (HMSO, 1991).

21 Kathleen McDermott and Roy D. King, 'Mind games: Where the action is in prisons', *The British Journal of Criminology* 28(3) (1988): 357–77 [p. 373].

22 Crewe, 'Depth, weight, tightness', p. 512.

23 Ben Jarman and Claudia Vince, *Making Progress? What Progression Means for People Serving the Longest Sentences* (PRT, 2022). HMI Prisons, *Annual Report 2022–23* (HMIP, 2023).

24 Erwin James, 'The real me', *The Guardian*, 24 April 2009, https://www.theguardian.com/society/2009/apr/24/erwin-james-journalism

25 Mr Walker, prisoner featured in BBC documentary series, *Parole*, (2023), https://www.bbc.co.uk/iplayer/episode/m001jw8y/parole-series-1-episode-3

26 James, 'The real me'.

27 Erwin James, *Redeemable: A Memoir of Darkness and Hope* (Bloomsbury, 2016), p. 330.

Chapter 7

1 Mathiesen, *Prison on Trial*.

2 E.g. see, Mary Speck, 'As El Salvador's gang crackdown continues, citizens wonder what's next?' United States Institute for Peace, 10 May 2023, https://www.usip.org/publications/2023/05/el-salvadors-gang-crackdown-continues-citizens-wonder-whats-next

3 Joel Feinberg, 'The expressive function of punishment', *The Monist* 49 (1965), pp. 397–423 [p. 403].

4 Esther van Ginneken, *The Pain and Purpose of Punishment: A Subjective Perspective*, Howard League What is Justice? Working Paper 22 (2016), https://howardleague.org/wp-content/uploads/2016/04/HLWP-22-2016.pdf

5 Omid Firouzi Tabar, Michele Miravalle, Daniela Ronco and Giovanni Torrente, *Reducing the Prison Population in Europe: Do Community Based Sentences Work?*, European Prison Observatory,

Alternatives to detention (Antigone Edizioni, 2016), http://www.prisonobservatory.org/upload/EPO_2_WS1_Final_report.pdf

6   Scottish Sentencing Council (2022) *Sentencing Young People: Sentencing Guideline* (Edinburgh: Scottish Government), p. 3, https://www.scottishsentencingcouncil.org.uk/media/2171/sentencing-young-people-guideline-for-publication.pdf

7   BBC News website, Teenage rapist's sentence condemned as 'not justice', 4 April 2023, https://www.bbc.co.uk/news/uk-scotland-edinburgh-east-fife-65173054

8   Davis, *Are Prisons Obsolete?*

9   Sarah Lamble, 'Bridging the gap between reformists and abolitionists: Can non-reformist reforms guide the work of prison inspectorates?', Institute for Crime and Justice Policy Research, 22 March 2022, https://www.icpr.org.uk/news-events/2022/bridging-gap-between-reformists-and-abolitionists-can-non-reformist-reforms-guide

10   Pat Carlen, 'Women's imprisonment: Models of reform and change', *Probation Journal* 49 (2002), pp. 76–87.

11   Carlen, 'Women's imprisonment', p. 86.

12   Ruth Mann, Flora Fitzalan Howard and Jenny Tew, 'What is a rehabilitative prison culture?', *Prison Service Journal* 235 (2018), pp. 3–9.

13   The CPT's minimum standard for living space per person in a multi-occupancy cell is 4 m^2 and the cell in Tripoli was approximately 80 m^2.

14   James Kilgore, 'Repackaging mass incarceration', *Counterpunch* (2014), https://www.counterpunch.org/2014/06/06/repackaging-mass-incarceration/

15   E.g., see First Step Alliance, 'What we can learn from Norway's prison system: Rehabilitation & recidivism', 2022, https://www.firststepalliance.org/post/norway-prison-system-lessons

16   Piers Hernu, 'Norway's controversial "cushy prison" experiment – could it catch on in the UK?', *Mail Online*, 25 July 2011, https://www.dailymail.co.uk/home/moslive/article-1384308/Norways-controversial-cushy-prison-experiment--catch-UK.html

17   Ugelvik and Damsa, 'The pains of crimmigration imprisonment'.

18   World Population Review, *Recidivism Rates by Country 2023*, https://worldpopulationreview.com/country-rankings/recidivism-rates-by-country

19   Tapio Lappi-Seppälä, 'Community sanctions as substitutes to imprisonment in the Nordic countries', in *Law and Contemporary*

Problems 82 (2019), pp. 17–50, https://scholarship.law.duke.edu/lcp/vol82/iss1/3

[20] Synøve N. Andersen and Kjetil Telle 'Better out than in? The effect on recidivism of replacing incarceration with electronic monitoring in Norway', *European Journal of Criminology* 19(1) (2019), pp. 55–76 [pp. 57–8].

[21] Andersen and Telle, 'Better out than in? The effect on recidivism of replacing incarceration with electronic monitoring in Norway'; Lappi-Seppälä, 'Community Sanctions as substitutes to imprisonment in the Nordic countries'.

[22] Albert W. Dzur, Ian Loader and Richard Sparks (eds), *Democratic Theory and Mass Incarceration* (Oxford University Press, 2016).

[23] Todd Clear, *Imprisoning Communities*.

[24] Amy E. Weaver and Vesla Mae Lerman, *Arresting Citizenship: The Democratic Consequences of American Crime Control* (University of Chicago Press, 2014), cited by Dzur, Loader and Sparks, *Democratic Theory and Mass Incarceration*, p. 8.

[25] This is based on the test for a well-functioning prison originally set by Phil Wheatley, a former Director General of Prisons for England and Wales. See *Prison Service Annual Report and Accounts: April 2000–March 2001*. HC29 (The Stationery Office, 2001), p. 27.

FURTHER READING

Michelle Alexander, *The New Jim Crow: Mass Incarceration in the Age of Colorblindness* (New Press, 2010).

Pat Carlen and Anne Worrall, *Analysing Women's Imprisonment* (2nd edition, Routledge, 2012).

Todd R. Clear, *Imprisoning Communities: How Mass Incarceration Makes Disadvantaged Neighborhoods Worse* (Oxford University Press, 2009).

Ben Crewe 'Depth, weight, tightness: Revisiting the pains of imprisonment', *Punishment & Society* 13 (2011), pp. 509–29.

Criminal Justice Inspectorates, *Neurodiversity in the Criminal Justice System: A Review of Evidence* (CJ Inspectorates, 2021), https://www.justiceinspectorates.gov.uk/cjji/inspections/neurodiversity-in-the-criminal-justice-system-a-review-of-evidence/

Seena Fazel and Katharina Seewald, 'Severe mental illness in 33,588 prisoners worldwide: Systematic review and meta-regression analysis', *The British Journal of Psychiatry* 200 (2012), pp. 364–73.

Michel Foucault, *Discipline and Punish: The Birth of the Prison* (Pantheon, 1977).

Natasha A. Frost and Todd R. Clear, 'Theories of mass incarceration', in John Wooldredge and Paula Smith (eds), *The Oxford Handbook of Prisons and*

Imprisonment (Oxford University Press, 2016), pp. 104–122.

David Garland, 'What is penal populism? Public opinion, expert knowledge, and penal policy-formation in democratic societies', in Alison Liebling, Joanna Shapland, Richard Sparks and Justice Tankebe (eds) *Crime, Justice, and Social Order: Essays in Honour of A.E. Bottoms* (Oxford Academic, 2022), pp. 249–72.

Mary Gibson, 'Global perspectives on the birth of the prison', *The American Historical Review* 116 (2011), pp. 1040–63.

Michael Ignatieff, 'State, civil society, and total institutions: A critique of recent social histories of punishment', *Crime and Justice* 3 (1981), pp. 153–92.

Erwin James, *Redeemable: A Memoir of Darkness and Hope* (Bloomsbury, 2016).

Tapio Lappi-Seppälä, 'The fall of the Finnish prison population', *Journal of Scandinavian Studies in Criminology and Crime Prevention* 1 (2000), pp. 27–40.

Fergus McNeill, 'Rehabilitation, corrections and society', Distinguished Scholar address to the ICPA conference, *Advancing Corrections Journal* 5 (2018), p. 18, http://eprints.gla.ac.uk/159625/7/159625.pdf

Daniel P. Mears and Joshua C. Cochran 'Who goes to prison?' in John D. Wooldredge and Paula Smith (eds), *The Oxford Handbook of Prisons and Imprisonment* (Oxford University Press, 2018), pp. 29–52.

Norval Morris and David J. Rothman (eds), *The Oxford History of the Prison: The Practice of Punishment in Western Society* (Oxford University Press, 1995).

Julian V. Roberts, Loretta J. Stalans, David Indermaur and Mike Hough, *Penal Populism and Public Opinion: Lessons from Five Countries* (Oxford University Press, 2003).

Jason Warr, '"Always gotta be two mans": Lifers, risk, rehabilitation, and narrative labour', *Punishment & Society* 22 (2020), pp. 28–47.

Albert Woodfox, *Solitary: Unbroken by Four Decades in Solitary Confinement. My Story of Transformation and Hope* (Text Publishing Company, 2019).

Lucia Zedner, 'Wayward sister: The prison for women', in Norval Morris and David J. Rothman (eds), *The Oxford History of the Prison: The Practice of Punishment in Western Society* (Oxford University Press, 1997), pp. 329–61.

INDEX

References to figures are in *italics*

INDEX

Damiens, Robert-François 27
Davis, Angela Y. 1, 35–6, 77,
   87, 125
debtors 19
decarceration 74–7, 124–5
democracy 66, 134–5
demonization 65–6
deterrence 7–8, 93–4, 120
Dickens, Charles 18, 20–1, 34
dignity in prison 105–9
Disabilities Trust (UK charity) 93
disenfranchisement of prisoners 135
drug misuse 73, 89, 92, 114–15
drugs policy 62–5
Dukakis, Mike 66
Dzur, Albert W. 134, 135

E

Eastern State Penitentiary,
   Pennsylvania 20–1, 34
Ehrlichman, John 63
El Salvador 122
electronic monitoring (EM) 133
England and Wales, prison
   statistics 37–8, 51, 69, 72,
   76–7, 85, 86–7, 88, 90–1
Epstein, Rona 85
European Committee for the
   Prevention of Torture (CPT) 54
European Enlightenment 24

F

Fair Sentencing Act (US) 64
family and community 50, 51,
   71–2, 84, 116
Feinberg, Joel 123
Finland 51, 74–7, 78, 134
first night in prison 1, 23, 97–102
foreign national prisoners 4–5,
   50, 56–7, 102–3, 104–5
Foucault, Michel 10, 18, 26–8,
   30–1, 33, 42–3, 49, 121–2
France 85

French colonialism 44–5
Frost, Natasha 71
Fry, Elizabeth 33
Fuchu Prison, Japan 49–51
furlough programmes 66

G

gang membership 72–4, 122
Garland, David 31, 62
Gerbner, Katharine 44
gulags 52–3

H

Haldeman, H.R. 63
health problems 5, 50, 56–7,
   71–2, 85–90, 104–5, 113–14
Hitchens, Peter 81–2
Horton, Willie 66
House of Commons Justice
   Committee (UK) 72
Howard, John 18, 19, 33
Howard, Michael 1

I

identity changes in prison 109–10
Ignatieff, Michael 18, 32–3
immigration detention 56–8
Indochina 44–5

J

James, Erwin 113, 115–16
Japan 40, 48–51
Jim Crow laws 13, 68–9

K

Kaufman, Emma 54, 56–7
Kenya 40, 42–3, 43, 46–8, 47,
   50, 107
King, Roy D. 112

L

Lamble, Sarah 127–8
Lappi-Seppälä, Tapio 74–5, 75–6